Learning to Learn

A GUIDE TO BECOMING INFORMATION LITERATE IN THE 21ST CENTURY

Second Edition

Ann Marlow Riedling

Neal-Schuman Publishers, Inc.

New York   London

KH

**Don't miss this book's
companion Web site
www.neal-schuman.com/learning
User name = learningtolearn
Password = infolit21**

Published by Neal-Schuman Publishers, Inc.
100 William St., Suite 2004
New York, NY 10038

Printed and bound in the United States of America.

The paper used in this publication meets the minimum requirements of American National Standard for Information Sciences—Permanence of Paper for Printed Library Materials, ANSI Z39.48-1992.∞

Library of Congress Cataloging-in-Publication Data

Riedling, Ann Marlow, 1952-
  Learning to learn : a guide to becoming information literate in the 21st century / Ann Marlow Riedling. — 2nd ed.
    p. cm.
  Includes bibliographical references and index.
  ISBN 1-55570-556-1 (alk. paper)
  1. Information literacy. 2. Information literacy—Problems, exercises, etc.
3. Research—Methodology. 4. Research—Methodology—Problems,
exercises, etc. 5. Electronic information resource searching. 6. Electronic
information resource searching—Problems, exercises, etc. 7. Report writing.
8. Report writing—Problems, exercises, etc. I. Title.
  ZA3075.R54 2006
  028.7—dc22

                                              2006013721

08/26/08

Table of Contents

List of Figures

List of Exercises

Foreword to the Second Edition

In the span of my career as a school library media specialist and communication skills instructor in a large suburban school district, I have seen the evolution of technology change the nature of librarianship and of learning in general. With each new stage, educators have creatively adapted instructional methods and technical procedures to best serve students' information needs. Currently, as Reference/Instruction Librarian at a small liberal arts university, I am delighted with Ann Marlow Riedling's second edition of *Learning to Learn*. My colleagues and I have used the first edition of *Learning to Learn* for several semesters, and all of the reasons we chose it as a textbook for our eight-week, online Information Literacy course in the first place are skillfully reinforced in the second edition.

Learning to Learn is perfectly suited for a broad range of learners, from secondary school to university levels. The second edition, however, will be especially popular with adult learners on the undergraduate level who have returned to school to pursue professional or personal goals, and who, for various reasons, have missed out on the technology that has evolved over the last two decades. The author's tone and approach toward becoming information literate alleviates their "panic" and offers concrete lessons that can be understood and applied to the higher level thinking activities incorporated throughout the text.

The author conveys a passion for the importance of information literacy in a motivational manner that engages students to take charge of their own learning. The content is thorough, accurate, and interactive. It is effectively related to career and real-life situations. The emphasis on academic honesty is admirable, and the chapters on plagiarism, copyright, and citation styles are valuable contributions that many "would-be" textbooks slight. The revisions, updates, and tools of the second edition greatly enhance its usability as a textbook and greatly enhance its adaptability to the online learning environment.

Online instructors of information literacy constantly strive to keep content fresh, current and interactive. This is no small task. It seems that this course is a constant work in progress; it is ever evolving due to the changing nature of information. Without a doubt, the strongest element of the second edition of *Learning to Learn* is the CD for instructors which will more easily facilitate designing an interactive course. The Power Point presentations on this resource will prove to be real time savers for instructors, streamlining hours of preparation time.

Overall, the second edition of *Learning to Learn* flows with a cohesiveness that makes it a very readable resource for students. Using it as a required text in an information-literacy course can provide students with the foundation needed to proceed on their own. In the beginning chapters of the book, Dr. Riedling gives the best working definition of information literacy I have yet to come across. She supports this definition with numerous examples of what information-literate people can actually do and how information literacy can benefit one in all walks of life. In addition, she succinctly explains four popular research models and the rationale behind each one. In the middle chapters, she enumerates the steps of the research process. Students will find this enumeration extremely valuable because it breaks down the seemingly overwhelming task of conducting research into manageable parts. In the final chapter, the author skillfully parallels the research process with the writing process. The expanded glossary will be helpful to students as they learn new vocabulary associated with information literacy. The substantial references for "Further Reading" and "Webliographies" placed at the end of each chapter will expand the usefulness of this book as a future reference with interdisciplinary application. The image of the library, both physical and virtual, is clearly portrayed as a place where readers will always come to write, writers will always come to read, and learners will always come to learn.

Peggy Ridlen, MLS
Assistant Professor and Reference/Instruction Librarian
Fontbonne University (Saint Louis, MO)

Foreword to the First Edition

Anyone who knows me knows that I am passionate in my work about two things: information literacy and libraries. I firmly believe that information literacy is essential to the success of everyone in our world, and that libraries are key institutions for ensuring that people become information literate. To me, information literacy is the 4th R; it's not enough anymore to be able to read, write, and do math. People need to be able to analyze their information needs and find, evaluate, and use the requisite information. That's what the Big6 approach to information and technology skills is all about, and we've got a long way to go to make information literacy learning a reality.

Learning to Learn is another step forward in the effort to make learning information skills an attainable goal. I am pleased to write this foreword to Ann Marlow Riedling's new book.

Learning to Learn succinctly lays out the steps and approaches to information literacy, from beginning to end. She writes, "Information literacy is the ability to access, evaluate, organize, and use information." To this end, *Learning to Learn* takes the reader from what it means to be information literate, through research planning, finding information, using information resources (for example, libraries and the Internet), evaluation, copyright and plagiarism, citation styles, to general writing skills.

At its center, being information literate means "understanding the how, what, why, when, and where about the information with which you are presented." As Ann Riedling recognizes, this is the evolving nature of our understanding about the marriage of information and learning. A true learner must be an information-literate person, and will continually add to their skills and abilities to conduct research—to frame questions as well as find and use information to resolve those questions.

Learning to Learn will be a valuable tool in the broad sense, but also in its ability to lead individual learners down the ever-widening path to information literacy. We're not talking here about the "fad of the month" that sometimes seems to pervade education and library work. *Learning to Learn* is enduring.

Michael B. Eisenberg

Michael B. Eisenberg (Ph.D., Syracuse University, MLS, State University of New York at Albany) is the Dean of the Information School at the University of Washington and a prolific author on the subject of information literacy. He is nationally known for creating the Big6 Skills, an innovative approach to teaching problem-solving, critical thinking and information and technology skills. For many years, Dr. Eisenberg was Director of the Information Institute of Syracuse, which includes the ERIC Clearinghouse on Information and Technology and the award-winning AskERIC service.

Preface

Learning to Learn: A Guide to Becoming Information Literate in the 21ˢᵗ Century, Second Edition, is designed to be a hands-on, step-by-step guide to becoming information literate. I designed this text for high school, community college, and college students who are first developing their research skills, as well as for adults returning to their studies after a long hiatus.

The first edition of *Learning to Learn: A Guide to Becoming Information Literate* provided an introductory information literacy text; this second edition, completely revised and updated, builds on that success; incorporating numerous instructor and student comments and requests. This new edition features:

- a larger variety of problem-solving models.
- more extensive webliographies (now provided at the end of each chapter).
- numerous new exercises.
- detailed explanatory figures to help illuminate obscure concepts;
- a thorough glossary of terms.
- extensive further readings.
- a wide assortment of some of the best, interactive research-oriented information literacy sites currently available on the Web;
- a highly integrated companion Web site providing direct links to the Web sites, all charts and figures, exercises, glossary of terms, and complete references. It also reproduces many of the exercises, making it easy to print them out or complete them on your computer;
- a CD for instructors that contains several PowerPoint presentations for instructional use, printable charts, figures and exercises, as well as useful instructional tips and strategies.

ORGANIZATION

The chapters in *Learning to Learn: A Guide to Becoming Information Literate in the 21st Century, Second Edition,* are arranged sequentially — each concept builds on those that have come before it. I recommend that you follow this order, but if you need help with a particular aspect of research, please go directly to the relevant chapter.

Chapter 1: "What Does It Mean to Be Information Literate?" lays the groundwork for the chapters that follow, providing a comprehensive explanation of what information literacy is and evaluating some of the ways it can be developed. In order to illustrate the research process, four prominent research models are discussed, offering an overview of how information literacy can be put to practice.

Chapter 2: "I Am Ready to Research. Where Do I Start?" discusses how to make your research as effective as possible by selecting a subject and a topic. This process of progressive specification will help clarify your thinking and assist you in the development of your own ideas.

Chapter 3: "How Do I Find the Information I Need?" explains how to design and implement a research process styled to meet your own needs. It first goes through the details of developing a search plan and then proceeds to look into how specific kinds of resources can serve your ideal ends.

Chapter 4: "How Can the Library (and Virtual Library) Help Me?" looks into how to best go about finding the resources you need once you have a general sense of what you are looking for. By presenting both the ideals that underlie libraries and the various services that they make available, this chapter serves to provide a useful overview of one of our world's most remarkable civic institutions. In a development new to this edition, it also looks into how you can also put the resources of digital libraries to work.

Chapter 5: "There Is So Much Information on the Internet. Where Do I Begin?" moves your search to the Web, discussing the value of various types of search engines, the difference between the visible and the invisible Web and various other fundamental tips. With this information at your fingertips you will find it much easier to quickly target and track down the best possible information.

Chapter 6: "How Do I Know If What I Read Is True?" explains how to evaluate the materials you discover as you go about doing your research. The guides in this chapter will provide strategies for gauging the worthiness of materials of all types, be they in print, online, or in some other alternate format. As the material in this chapter will demonstrate, such critical thinking and analysis is an indispensable part of the information-literacy picture.

Chapter 7: "What Should I Know About Plagiarism and Copyright?" delves into the ethical dimension of research, describing how and why you should work to avoid stealing others' ideas and work. In the process, it also discusses protections on your own output, be it artistic, academic, or otherwise.

Chapter 8: "How Do I Give Credit to the Creator of the Information I Read?" shows how you can give formal credit to others when you make use of their work. In particular, it explains three basic citation styles: *Chicago Manual of Style, MLA Handbook for Writers of Research Papers,* and *Publication Manual of the American Psychological Association.* Attention is also given to the creation of annotated bibliographies and the proper means of placing citations within a text.

Chapter 9: "Now That I've Finished the Research, How Do I Write the Paper?" provides methods, guidelines, and examples to assist you with organizing research information. Among other things, this chapter walks through outlining, writing a rough draft, making revisions, improving writing, and presenting research—all important aspects of high-quality research.

I hope this new edition of *Learning to Learn: A Guide to Becoming Information Literate in the 21st Century* will become a trusted and constant companion as you master the skills of information literacy.

A Note to Instructors

Like the first edition, the second edition of *Learning to Learn: A Guide to Becoming Information Literate in the 21st Century* is meant to guide learners at all levels on their journeys to information literacy. While the practical advice and exercises are designed to enable self-directed learning, it is also my hope that the book can be a powerful tool for teaching. This edition is suitable for a wide range of basic information-literacy classes, ranging from junior and senior high school through community college and freshman college classes. Many of the new elements of this edition have been tailored to fit the requests of instructors who have used the book. *Learning to Learn,* Second Edition, will provide students with the basics of information literacy, information access, research, using today's libraries, evaluation of resources, copyright and plagiarism, basic citation styles, and much more to strive and thrive in today's increasingly complicated world of information gathering.

My first goal for both editions was to create a useful and valuable tool to help all readers interface with our increasingly sophisticated information society. This second edition tries to reflect and respond to the remarkable rate at which our modern world changes. Additional problem-solving models, exercises, figures, and further readings are provided. In addition, new Web sites are included within the text and in chapter "Webliographies." Most importantly, the second edition is designed to interface with a companion web site for students and a CD-ROM for instructors. The instructor CD-ROM increases the practical value of the text, providing printable exercises, figures, further readings, Webliographies and other important "tid-bits" of practical, helpful information regarding various aspects of information literacy and research. Using the resources on the web site, students can print out copies of the charts, tables, and exercises found throughout the text, making it easy to take advantage of the book's resources in a wide variety of settings and circumstances. The instructor CD-ROM is designed to make instruction easier and to provide tools, tips, and strategies for effective teaching. It also contains exciting PowerPoint presentations for your use in teaching. Expand or modify any of the content to better support your own instructional needs or simply use it as a spring board for developing ideas related to your own lesson plans. Remember, you are only limited by your imagination!

The second edition of *Learning to Learn* presents the entire range of research and information literacy in a workable way. It is my sincere hope that it will both provide engaging experiences in its own right and increase the level of your students' appreciation for, and engagement with, their studies and scholarship.

Acknowledgments

There are six special people I want to thank for this book:

Thank you, Charles Harmon, Director of Publishing, Neal-Schuman Publishers, Inc., for believing in me and the importance of this book.

Thank you, Michael Kelley, Development and Production Editor, Neal-Schuman Publishers, Inc., for absolutely brilliant and insightful editing, as well as support and encouragement that cannot be matched.

Thank you, Peggy Ridlen, for the kind foreword to this edition.

Thank you, Russ, my husband, who provides me with constant assistance, total and unending support and encouragement for all of my endeavors, and the patience of Job. He inspires me to be what I am.

Thank you, Marlow, my daughter, who understands my long hours of work and has constant faith in what I do. She is sunshine every day.

A very special thank you to Jacob Brogan, Editorial Assistant, Neal-Schuman Publishers, Inc., for superb editing, unbelievable patience, and ongoing encouragement and support in the preparation of this book's second edition.

Without these people, this book would not have been possible . . . and thank God it is, because I believe in it with all my heart. May all who read it understand how to learn and to move forward in the twenty-first century.

Chapter 1

What Does It Mean to Be Information Literate?

INTRODUCTION

With each passing year, the ways we seek out, access, and process information grow more sophisticated. Research is no longer a simple matter of asking the right questions or reading the right books—today there are countless sources of knowledge, each of them serving different needs. While many today think they need do no more than plug a few words into Google to learn what they want to know, accessing the full range and diversity of the information that is available on any one topic takes a little more work. Navigating the vast sea of information sources available today is a crucial skill both in the classroom and out of it. Sometimes we all feel that we are drowning in information, but if we take seriously the need to swim through it, the reward is always worth the effort. Before we can learn anything new, we first have to learn to learn.

Over time, numerous "literacies" have developed. Today, simply learning to read is no longer enough—we must be able to make sense of all the data sent to us by our environment, whether it comes from a painting, a book, or a computer screen. The ability to access, evaluate, organize, and use information is called information literacy. Information comes in a wide variety of formats (books, videotapes, CD-ROMs, etc.) and is accessible by numerous means. Whether at the library or on a home Internet connection, we now have access to a vast array of databases and digital materials that few could have imagined 30 years ago. At the same time, older information sources are not going away, and we still must know how to search through print encyclopedias and scholarly books. Information literacy is not just about the ability to use these various media. It is about figuring out how to find balance between them, figuring out what to use and when to use it. In the modern information environment, it is more crucial than ever to distinguish between fact and fiction, to seek out quality materials over the enormous quantity of available possibilities To *learn to learn* you will have to develop these and other skills, transforming the way you make knowledge your own.

Given practice and experience, everyone develops personal information—literacy strategies. This chapter will discuss four common research models to provide perspective on the ways some people look for and use information. Remember that no one way of doing things works for everyone, so try not to worry if none of these models seem right for you. In future chapters we will deal with the specifics of research and writing, allowing you to make your own path to information literacy.

INFORMATION LITERACY

What Does Information Literacy Really Mean?

According to the most famous maxim of the scientist and philosopher Francis Bacon, "Knowledge is power." By this, Bacon did not mean that knowledge was a source of political dominance or control, but that knowing a thing was a good in itself. Knowledge, Bacon felt, begets knowledge, with each lesson learned making it easier for us to learn others. Though he lived centuries before the appearance of computers and the Internet, Bacon had learned the lessons of information literacy well.

First, it is important to understand that information literacy forms the basis for lifelong learning. It is common to all disciplines, to all learning environments, and to all levels of education. Information literacy enables you to master content, become more self-directed, and assume greater control over your own learning. The abilities to access, comprehend, and use information have become the skills you must develop in order to function in today's world.

A number of people and organizations have developed definitions of information literacy. According to the American Library Association (1989), information literacy is the ability to access, evaluate, organize, and use information from a variety of sources. Being information literate requires that

- you know how to clearly define a subject or area of investigation.
- you select the appropriate terminology to express the concept or subject under investigation.

- you formulate a search strategy that takes into consideration different sources of information and the various ways that information is organized.
- you analyze the data collected for value, relevancy, quality, and suitability, and you subsequently turn that information into knowledge.

This involves a deeper understanding of how and where to locate information, the ability to judge whether the information is meaningful and, ultimately, how best that information can be incorporated to address the problem or issue at hand.

With the rapid increase in the amount of information and the increasing availability of information technology, information literacy has quickly become one of the most vital sets of skills for the twenty-first century. What does that mean for *you*? It means that you can proficiently use an online library catalog; you understand how to effectively search for information on the Internet; you know how to use a computer successfully; you understand that not everything is "free for the taking" (there are copyright laws); you can "think outside of the box"—critically and individually; and you can competently express what you think and write to others.

Information literate people can

- locate information by recognizing the need for information, understanding that accurate and complete information is the basis for intelligent decision making.
- form questions based on information needs.
- develop successful search strategies.
- efficiently and effectively access print and electronic materials.

Information is available from a variety of resources, including online library databases, electronic magazines, the Internet, books, magazines, journals, and so forth. As an information-literate person, you must know why, how, and when to use all of these resources effectively and efficiently. Currently, little doubt remains that information literacy is increasingly important in order for you to function in diverse information and communication environments, as both a consumer and a producer. Many people are now comfortable with technology, although the extents of information authorship, ownership, and creation elude them. Blending the skills and abilities from media, computer, visual, and cultural literacy, information literacy is a necessary competency for the twenty-first century.

Let's look at information literacy from a more practical standpoint. As an information-literate person, what exactly do *you* need to be able to do? The following list includes both information-literacy skills and an example that shows each one in use.

- Determine the extent of information needed.
  (*For example, you might choose Canadian immigration as your research topic.*)
- Access the needed information effectively and efficiently.
  (*You know to use proper search words—e.g., "Immigration, laws, Canada"—when searching for information or locating an online article or book about the issue.*)
- Evaluate information and its sources critically.
  (*You realize that* not *all information on the Internet is fact—and are able to distinguish fact from fiction.*)
- Incorporate selected information into one's knowledge base.
  (*You comprehend this information—really understand what you are saying.*)
- Use information effectively to accomplish a specific task.
  (*You write about immigration laws in Canada based on the resources and information you have located—from numerous sources.*)
- Understand the legal and socioeconomic issues surrounding the use of information—access and use information ethically and legally.
  (*You understand that what you say can have legal implications— you understand copyright, plagiarism, and the effects of the "printed word."*)

According to Gerry McGovern (2001), the publisher of *New Thinking,* a newsletter covering Web-publishing topics, if you are an information-literate person you

- recognize and understand the value of information.
- read a lot, are inquisitive, and are always willing to learn.
- have the ability to isolate where new information is required to solve a problem.
- feel comfortable using information technology.
- have the ability to locate content resources efficiently and effectively.
- have the ability to evaluate content critically and competently.
- have the ability to use content accurately and creatively.
- have the ability to create quality content.

- are independent-minded but realize that collaboration is the best way to acquire and develop knowledge.
- have the ability to communicate what you know in an effective manner.

Good decisions depend on good information. Decision makers of all types must develop perceptive information skills if they are to prosper in our technological, global society. Being information-smart means knowing when you need help and where to find it. A truly information-literate person will know that real information power is having the right information when you need it. The most important thing, in other words, is not subject-specific skills, but a universal skill—that of using knowledge and its systematic acquisition as the foundation for performance, skill, and achievement.

Why Is Information Literacy Important Now?

At a conference of U.S. governors in 2005, Microsoft co-founder Bill Gates called the high schools of the United States obsolete. He argued that elected officials should be ashamed of a system that leaves millions of students unable to meet the demands that will confront them in the future. As Gates rightly puts it, an education that does not teach us how to interface with our world is no education at all.

Because of resources like the Internet, finding high-quality information is now harder than ever, **not** easier. Finding the "good stuff" is not always quick. And the good stuff does not always come cheaply, either. To make matters worse, just because you know how to use a particular information technology today does not mean that there is not another one right behind it that you will have to learn how to use tomorrow!

In fact, one of the most important pieces of the information-literacy puzzle is a willingness to adapt to emerging forms of conveying knowledge. Just as a printed book is not always the fastest or best way of finding information today, new formats and media are constantly coming into vogue, each with their own strengths and weaknesses. For example, at present blogs (short for Web logs)—highly subjective online sites in which authors discuss, analyze, and report on current events and other phenomena, often as they are happening—have become a significant part of the news-making process. Because they often have different levels of access, different kinds of knowledge, and different degrees of editorial constraint from those of conventional print journalists, blog writers often have very different perspectives on developing stories from the more traditional news media. Increasingly, paying attention to these new sources is a crucial means to a fuller understanding of the world in which we live. Even so, you would be likely to end up misinformed if you were to try to get all of your news from blogs alone. As with any novelty, the important thing to remember is that value is always a product of moderation. While new means to learning can be powerful tools, they should never be seen as outright replacements for all that has come before.

Much the same is true with regards to another relatively new form of conveying information on the Internet, the communally edited and written databases known as wikis. At present, the most famous wiki is the massive online encyclopedia known as Wikipedia. Because its entries are written by its readers, who may or may not be experts in their chosen topics, much of the information on this Web site is suspect and is not generally considered as reliable as material found in a more traditional encyclopedia, such as the *World Book*. Despite this, the immediacy of access and the diversity of the community behind it often makes Wikipedia's content more timely and comprehensive than that in more conventional sources. With good reason, Wikipedia is generally not accepted as a valid source in scholastic research, but it can be a great jumping off point when you know relatively little about a topic and want to figure out where you should begin. As with blogs, the important thing is to recognize how these wikis might be incorporated with more traditional sources to help broaden your horizon of understanding.

Our information society is perpetually mutating and expanding, and you will have to develop new skills if you hope to change with it. Although you cannot anticipate what other new technologies and formats the future will bring, you can strive to respond to them thoughtfully as they arrive on the scene. Further, many of the information-literacy strategies that will be introduced in this book apply to new ways of learning as fully as they do to the old. In other words, no matter how the tools to learn change, the ways you learn will remain much the same. Thus, it will always be important to evaluate your sources (Chapter 6), avoid plagiarizing the work of others (Chapter 7), and so on.

Today's employers are looking for people who understand and can adapt to the characteristics of the Information Age. If a student has *learned how to learn,* he or she is a much more attractive job candidate. An information-literate individual—with his or her strong analytical, critical thinking, and problem-solving skills—can be expected to be an adaptable, capable, and valuable employee with much to contribute.

Exercise 1.1: Information Literacy

Visit the following Web site and proceed through the tutorial. "Texas Information Literacy Tutorial (TILT)"

- http://tilt.lib.utsystem.edu

This interactive tutorial helps you to explore and research in the online world. The TILT tutorial is divided into different sections in order to generate examples relevant to your interests. While exploring each section, consider the following questions:

- Censorship and freedom of speech: "With people from different countries and of all ages on the Internet, should there be consideration of what is appropriate for everybody?"
- Global communities: "How will online communities deal with spamming, flaming, and unwanted solicitations?"
- Internet business: "How are businesses evolving to target the online community and to meet the demands of new technologies?"
- Laws and regulations: "What should be regulated on the Internet?"
- New trends: "Will it be a better future or a science-fiction nightmare?"
- Security and privacy: "Is there privacy in an online world? What kind of information is safe to share over the Internet?"

Information Literacy involves some very "hot" topics. You are the future . . . and you will assist in formulating the answers to these questions.

Now, pair up with another person and debate one of these questions/issues. Gather as much information as you can about "your point of view." For example, if you believe that there should be regulations on the Internet, find out if other people believe this too and why. Justify your argument. Remember, there are two sides to every story.

PROBLEM-SOLVING MODELS

Knowledge seeking is a process. It is applicable to information in any form. Self-directed learning skills are critical in your development as a lifelong, independent person. Mastering a research model (like one of the four discussed in this chapter) introduces you to research processes and problem-solving skills—necessities for lifelong learning. Remember that the model you "adopt" is likely to shift as you mature in your own learning styles and abilities. You should not feel like you have to take up a single way of doing research and follow it without question. Research models exist as guidelines, not as hard and fast rules. If any of the strategies below seem particularly intriguing to you, investigate the Webliography at the end of this chapter to find out more. While there are a variety of means to approach research, four well-regarded systems are discussed here: *Big6*, ISP, I-Search, and Flip-It.

The Big6 Skills Model

A prominent problem-solving/research-process model is *The Big6*, developed by Michael Eisenberg and David Berkowitz (2000). The *Big6* model makes it easier to see the connection between the research process and using Internet information sources effectively. This approach focuses on the process of solving information problems and brings all information to the forefront. It is a systematic approach, and this well-known model is being taught widely as a guide for research. Here is the "basic model" of the *Big 6*:

1. Task definition
   a. Define the problem
   b. Define the information requirements of the problem
2. Information-seeking strategies
   a. Determine the range of possible resources
   b. Evaluate the different possible resources to determine priorities
3. Location and access
   a. Locate sources
   b. Find information within resources
4. Use of information
   a. Engage with the source
   b. Extract information from a source
5. Synthesis
   a. Organize information from multiple sources
   b. Present information
6. Evaluation
   a. Judge the product
   b. Judge the information problem-solving process

Think of this practically. You need a car. You only have x amount of money to purchase a car. What do you do? The following are probable steps:

- You have already defined the problem—the need for a car.
- You gather information about the problem (cars under x amount of money available for purchase).
- You determine possible resources (advertisements, people, newspapers, etc.).
- You locate possible materials about available cars (purchase a newspaper, call a mechanic, visit a friend).
- You use the information about the location of possible cars that you can purchase by visiting the locations (used car lots, homes).
- You look at what you have seen (a 1996 Nissan for x amount, a 2003 Ford for x amount, and so on).
- You make a decision according to the information you have and buy the car—*based* on the information you have gathered.
- Later you may perhaps evaluate it. Does the car run properly? Have you seen cars for less money of the same type? Do you know what to "do better" the next time you look for a car?

 Exercise 1.2: *Big6*

Everyone has a need or interest of some nature (wishing to purchase a new computer or water heater, deciding where to go on vacation this summer, finding out more about a disease that a family member has, learning about hurricane paths near one's residence, and so forth). Using Figure 1.1, fill in the blanks with appropriate information. Share this figure with classmates and your instructor.

---

1. What is the problem you want to solve?	
2. What types of resources do you need to solve this problem? *(for example, books, interviews, online journal articles, Internet sources, videos, etc.)*	
3. Make an organized list of the best resources you located.	
4. Read and create written annotations for each resource.	
5. Extract the precise information you will use; write this down.	
6. Do you think you did an effective job of finding the resources needed? Explain.	
7. Do you believe that you located these efficiently? Explain.	

Figure 1.1   The *Big6*

The ISP Model

The Information Search Process (ISP) model was developed by Carol Kuhlthau (2002). This model is unique because it is based on research; it is also based on observations of "information seekers" involved in a research task. Kuhlthau identifies six "thinking" activities students engage in as they progress from topic selection through organization and preparation for writing.

1. Initiating a research assignment
2. Selecting a topic

3. Exploration information
4. Formulating a focus
5. Collecting information
6. Preparing to present

One of the most interesting aspects of this process is the way Kuhlthau's work emphasizes the attitudes and behaviors of students during the process. She explains that students begin to search for information because they want to know more about something that is interesting or troubling. In such cases, the motivation to seek information arises naturally out of the person's own experience. Although the ISP model appears linear, Kuhlthau argues that in practice students engage the stages recursively, revisiting activities typical of the earlier phases of the process if their topics turn out to be too narrow or too broad, if their foci change, or if they have difficulty finding information or resources.

 Exercise 1.3: ISP

Your instructor has given you an assignment; you are to use the ISP Model to discover the answer. This is the assignment. Use the following figure to assist you with this research: Recently, Sony released a series of music CDs that installed a copy-protection program known as a "rootkit" onto the computers of users. Though it was meant to protect Sony's copyrights, this software inadvertently made it easier for hackers to break into the computers of others. Based on your research, was this activity of the hackers legal . . . ethical . . . moral . . . . what you would do? Be explicit.

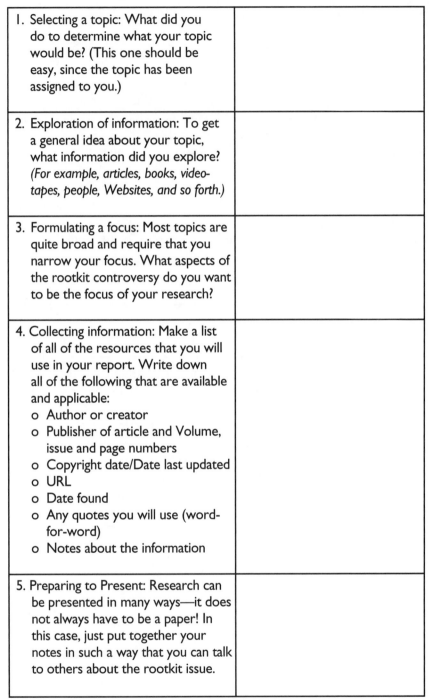

1. Selecting a topic: What did you do to determine what your topic would be? (This one should be easy, since the topic has been assigned to you.)	
2. Exploration of information: To get a general idea about your topic, what information did you explore? *(For example, articles, books, video-tapes, people, Websites, and so forth.)*	
3. Formulating a focus: Most topics are quite broad and require that you narrow your focus. What aspects of the rootkit controversy do you want to be the focus of your research?	
4. Collecting information: Make a list of all of the resources that you will use in your report. Write down all of the following that are available and applicable: o Author or creator o Publisher of article and Volume, issue and page numbers o Copyright date/Date last updated o URL o Date found o Any quotes you will use (word-for-word) o Notes about the information	
5. Preparing to Present: Research can be presented in many ways—it does not always have to be a paper! In this case, just put together your notes in such a way that you can talk to others about the rootkit issue.	

Figure 1.2   ISP

The I-Search Model

The I-Search Model, developed by Ken Macrorie in 1988, is unique in that the focus of research activity is a topic students choose entirely on the basis of a personal interest or connection. This model is an approach to research that uses the power of student interests, builds a personal understanding of the research process, and encourages stronger student writing. This model also stresses metacognitive thinking—that is, thinking about thinking. The I-Search process involves four central tasks:

1. Selecting a topic: Students explore their own interests through webbing activities and discussions with parents, peers, and teachers, as well as skimming and scanning resources in the library media center.
2. Researching the topic: This involves the generation of research questions, background reading, the creation of bibliographies, and student-conducted interviews.
3. Using the information found: This includes "highlighting" and taking notes. Reflection is encouraged at this stage through conferencing and the use of learning logs.
4. Completing the project: This includes the opportunity to share the experience and the project with peers.

Overall, the I-Search Process creates an "authentic" instructional environment.

 Exercise 1.4: I-Search

You are to choose an article that interests you. Please re-read this article; then pose a focused, researchable question based on what else you would like to learn about the subject of the article. (Use at lease one additional source to find the answer to your question—encyclopedia, interview, etc.). Prepare a short presentation for your fellow classmates and instructor. Include the following:

1) Title and source of the article
2) Your question and why you were interested
3) What you used to gather information
4) What you discovered
5) What it means to you

Prepare your presentation and display it to fellow classmates and your instructor. Remember . . . be specific about your sources!

The Flip-It! Model

The Flip-It! Model, developed by Alice H. Yucht, provides a four-stage guide to research grounded in learning theories and based on her own observations of students seeking information in school libraries. The Flip-It label is itself a mnemonic device that reminds students of important steps in the research task:

F (Focus on the topic)

L (Linking new information to what students know)

I (Interpretation of information)

P (Putting the final research project together)

"I-T" stands for "If" "Then," which represents a reflective questioning syntax, "If you know x then your next step is y.

 Exercise 1.5: Flip-It!

You have just completed a lesson about the effects of drinking alcoholic beverages—what it does to the body. Your teacher has now asked you to research the effects of drinking alcoholic beverages on car accidents and deaths. Using the Flip-It! Model below, discuss your new research topic.

F (Focus on topic): What specifically are you going to research? *(For example, what happens to the brain to cause accidents? How many automobile accidents are alcohol related?)*

L (Linking new information to what students know): How can you use what you learned about the effects of drinking alcoholic beverages to your new research topic? Be specific.

I (Interpretation of information): You have read new information. Write what it all means to you—an outline or rough draft is fine.

P (Putting the final research project together): Create a final research project—paper, presentation, or the like.

"I-T" stand for "If" "Then," which represents a reflective questioning syntax, "If you know x, then your next step is y. *If you know the effects of drinking alcoholic beverages on the functions of the body, is it easier to conduct research about alcohol and automobile accidents? Why or why not?*

CONCLUSION

No other change has offered greater challenges than the emergence of the Information Age. In an information society, you should have the right to information that can enhance your life. To reap the benefits of our global, technological society, you must be information literate. Our evolving world includes an incredible growth of knowledge, an explosion of technology, and a speedy reconfiguration of the boundaries that separate the enormous number of academic fields and social conventions. This complex society continues to expand at a rate beyond the capacity of individuals to comprehend. Collectively, and with the use of technologies that have potentiated the momentum of change, humanity generates tremendous amounts of information. Access to information is vital to ease the burden of change and to help society navigate its course toward the future. The abilities to access, comprehend, evaluate, and use information have become the skills you must develop in order to function in our world today. To become information literate is to *learn to learn!*

REFERENCES AND FURTHER READING

American Association of School Librarians and Association for Educational Communications and Technology. 1998. *Information Power: Guidelines for School Library Media Programs*. Chicago: American Library Association.

Barren, Daniel D. 2001. "Thanks for the Connections . . . Now Are We Information Literate?" *School Library Media Activities Monthly*, 18: 49.

Boyle, Ann. 2005. "A Formula for Successful Technology Integration Must Include Curriculum." *MultiMedia & Internet@Schools*, 12: 1.

Eisenberg, Michael B., and Robert E. Berkowitz. 2000. *The Big6 Collection: The Best of the Big6 Newsletter*. Worthington, OH: Linworth.

Eisenberg, M., C. Lowe, C. and K. Spitzer. 2004. *Information Literacy: Essential Skills for the Information Age* (2nd edition). Englewood, CO: Libraries Unlimited.

Ercegovac, Zorona. 2001. *Information Literacy, Search Strategies, Tools and Resources for High School Students*. Worthington, OH: Linworth.

Farmer, Lesley S. J. 2002. "Harnessing the Power of Information Power." *Teacher Librarian*, 29: 3.

Gates, Bill. 2005 February 26. "National Education Summit on High Schools: Prepared Remarks by Bill Gates, Co-chair." Available at http://www.gates foundation.org/MediaCenter/Speeches/BillgSpeeches/BGSpeechNGA-050226.htm.

Grassian, Esther, and Joan Kaplowitz. 2001. *Information Literacy Instruction: Theory and Practice*. New York: Neal-Schuman Publishers.

Haycock, Ken. 2004. "Metacognition, Models, Students, Learning." *Teacher Librarian*, 32: 1.

Irving, Ann. 1985. *Study Skills Across the Curriculum*. London: Educational Books.

Johnson, Doug. 2004. "Turning the Page." *School Library Journal* (November) 50: 11.

Joyce, Marilyn Z., and Julie I. Tallman. 2006. *Making the Writing and Research Connection with the I-Search Process* (2nd ed.). New York: Neal-Schuman Publishers.

Kuhlthau, Carol C. 2002. *Teaching the Library Research Process: A Step-By-Step Program for Secondary School Students* (2nd ed). New York: Scarecrow.

Martin, A., and H. Rader (Eds.) 2003. *Information Literacy and IT Literacy: Enabling Learning in the 21st Century*. New York: Neal-Schuman.

McGovern, Gerry. 2001. "Age of the Information Literate." *New Thinking Newsletter*. February 12, 2001. Available at *http://www.gerrymcgovern.com/nt/2001/nt_2001_02_12_information_literate.htm*.

Misakian, Jo Ellen Priest. 2004. *Information Literacy: Essential Skills for the Information Age* (2nd ed.). Englewood, CO: Libraries Unlimited.

Murphy, Paula. 2002. "A 21st Century Challenge: Preparing 'Cut and Paste' Students to be 'Information Literate' Citizens." *UC TLtC News & Events*.

Riedling, Ann Marlow. 2005. *What Does Information Literacy Look Like in the School Library Media Center?* Englewood, CO: Libraries Unlimited.

Shannon, D. 2002. "Kuhlthau's Information Search Process." *Library Trends*, 45: 4.

Snavely, Loanne. 2004. "Making Problem-Based Learning Work: Institutional Challenges." *Libraries and the Academy*, 4: 4.

Spence, Larry. 2004. "The Usual Doesn't Work: Why We Need Problem-Based Learning." *Libraries and the Academy*, 4: 4.

Thomas, Nancy Pickering. 2004. *Information Literacy and Information Skills Instruction: Applying Research to Practice in the Library Media Center* (2nd ed.). Westport, CT: Libraries Unlimited.

Thurlow, Crispin, Laura Lengel, and Alice Tomic. 2004. *Computer Mediated Communication: Social Interaction and the Internet*. CA: Sage.

Warlick, David. 2004. *Redefining Literacy for the 21st Century*. Worthington, OH: Linworth.

Young, Jeffrey R. 2004. "Testing Service to Unveil an Assessment of Computer and Information Literacy." *The Chronicle of Higher Education*, 51: 12.

Yucht, Alice H. 1997. FLIP IT! An Information Skills Strategy for Student Researchers. Worthington, OH: Linworth. (Although published in 1997, this is a useful article regarding the research model, FLIP-IT!)

WEBLIOGRAPHY

Research/Problem-Solving Models

Content literacy: The I-Search in Action
www.literacymatters.org/content/isearch/action.htm
This site shows how the I-Search model is used in "real life situations."
Information Inquiry for Teachers: ISP Model
http://eduscapes.com/info/isp.html
The ISP model is unique because it is based on research.
Information Literacy for the Information Age
www.big6.com
This Web site offers a wealth of information about the research process, Big6.
The I-Search Process
http://eduscapes.com/info/isearch.html
The key element of the I-Search is that students select topics of personal interest; it also stresses metacognitive thinking.
Nuts and Bolts of the *Big6:* In Search of Information Literacy
www.kn.pacbell.com/wired/big6
This site states that information in and of itself has no meaning, but applied properly and in context, it is one of the most powerful tools of humankind.
Pathways to Knowledge
http://eduscapes.com/info/pathways.html
This problem-solving/research model's focus is a nonlinear process for finding, using, and evaluating information.
Reading for information: The Trash-n-Treasure Method of Teaching Note Taking (Grades 3–12)
www.big6.com/showarticle.php?id=45
As stated in the Web site, "The real skill of note-taking lies not in the manual techniques for arranging material on a page, but in the cognitive techniques for looking for and asking relevant questions. Knowing what is important means knowing what it is important for having a sense of purpose" (Irving, 1985).
The Seven Steps of the Research Process
www.library.cornell.edu/okuref/research/skill1.htm
This Web site discusses a simple and effective strategy for finding information for a research paper and documenting the sources found.

General Information-Literacy Web Sites

Awesome News
www.awesomelibrary.org/news.html
This Web site offers *World News, USA News, News by Country, News for Kids and Teens,* and so forth.
eSkills UNE
www.une.edu.au/library/infolit/index.htm

The eSkills site is a step-by-step tutorial that guides one through the process of finding and using information for assignments and other assessment tasks.

Information Skills Resources on the Internet

www.iasl-slo.org/infoskills.html

This site includes links to a wealth of Web sites relating to information literacy and similar areas.

Newspapers in Education

www.newspapers.com

This site offers over 10,000 newspapers online.

Nine standards of information literacy, from *Information Power: Building Partnerships for Learning*

www.ala.org/aasl/ip_nine.html

This site, written by the American Library Association and the American Association of School Librarians, includes an in-depth discussion of the nine standards of information literacy.

Teacher-made Activities: Serious Fun with Research

http://teacher.scholastic.com/lessonrepro/lessonplans/theme/res48.htm

This site claims to have some of the best research activities/lesson plans on the Web.

Chapter 2

I Am Ready to Research.
Where Do I Start?

No matter how "brilliant" we are, many of us are not experienced researchers. We may be proud of the number of hits we receive from a search engine, for example, but often we become frustrated or end up resorting to surfing from one unhelpful site to next in the hopes of discovering the "one golden nugget." On other occasions we may start out excited about the wealth of information available in a library, only to throw up our hands in frustration when it comes to actually sorting through all the available books. Sometimes, we feel like abandoning our search outright, feeling unable find anything on our topic.

Part of the problem is that we often have difficulty defining exactly what kind of information we need. We imagine that it is difficult to figure out where we should begin and what we should look for. Often we do not even know how to focus on a topic and find literature pertaining to it. Further, we usually do not know enough about specific disciplines to choose a focused avenue of research and to develop a manageable research question.

Exploring information resources efficiently and critically evaluating results are information-literacy skills that are vital to today's world. If we know how to use information resources and recognize the characteristics and purposes of resources, we have a great advantage when working to understand something better. This gives us a firm foundation for future course work, but it also helps improve our everyday lives. While the discussion in this book will mostly be in terms of the classroom, information literacy affects every part of our lives. When we are trying to decide what product to buy, which school to apply to, or anything else we might not yet know, it is crucial that we know where to look. Informed decisions start with quality information, and with the materials in this chapter and those that follow it, you will learn how to make this a reality.

The research process is constantly evolving. The skills needed to learn about the best cars to buy or best banks in which to put our money have changed drastically over the years, and they will likely change further as the Internet and other technologies mutate in ways as of yet unknown. The only way to be sure that we will be ready for the information climate of tomorrow is to familiarize ourselves fully with the information-literacy skills of today. Of all the steps of learning to learn, few are more important than the need to

- differentiate between a subject and a topic;
- generate ideas for a research topic and decide on a topic;
- develop a thesis statement;
- become aware of where and how to locate resources for that specific topic;
- learn to focus;
- collect useful, accurate information; and
- utilize various tools and techniques for successful writing.

Writing a research paper or collecting the information that you need to make an important personal financial decision can be quite intimidating. It helps to break the process down into steps. This chapter will guide you through these steps and get you started.

SUBJECTS AND TOPICS

A *subject* is an expansive area of interest. Examples of subjects are education, sports, animals, medicine, and so forth. These subjects are much too large to research effectively. Therefore, you must narrow the large area (subject) to a smaller area (topic). Selecting a topic is an integral phase of the research process and it requires careful consideration and time. A *topic* can be thought of as a particular question, issue, problem, or concern within a given subject. For example, you might narrow down the subject of education to the topic of home schooling. Another example is the broad subject of violence, which can be narrowed to smaller subjects such as gun control, gangs, or school violence. In order to conduct successful research, you should begin with a topic that is not too large (you might be overwhelmed with information and not know where to begin) nor too small (you could have difficulty finding enough information on the topic). Choosing topics will become easier with practice.

DISCOVERING IDEAS AND DECIDING ON A TOPIC

Information is all around us. Finding information is not the problem; selecting the best and most relevant information from all that is available is the difficulty. The first step is to think about a topic that you find interesting or something you would like to learn more about. Your selected topic should also provide you with an opportunity to explore, do original thinking, and make judgments. It is wise to avoid topics for which only limited information is available and topics that are overworked (i.e., topics many people have already written about). When defining your topic, the following four questions may help direct you:

1. Do you have a definition of your topic in a dictionary, encyclopedia, or the Internet (for example, home AND schooling)? Find one and write it down.
2. Is the definition different from your understanding of the topic? Write down what is new to you.
3. What is not clear to you in the definition?
4. Are there any terms or ideas that you do not fully understand in the definition? List them.

It may also be helpful to visit a library and answer the following questions before deciding on your topic:

1. How many titles are listed about the topic in the catalog?
2. Is the topic broken down into subheadings in the catalog? It may be beneficial to list any subheadings that you can find.
3. How many articles can you locate on the topic? Try a number of online databases to see what you can locate. (See Chapter 4 for further information concerning online databases.)
4. How much information can you find on the Internet? Try a variety of search words (synonyms) and several different search engines and subject directories. (See Chapter 5 for further information about search engines and subject directories.)

Where you begin is critical to determining where you will end and how strong your research will be. Everyone approaches decision making in different ways. You bring your own experiences to the task when selecting topics. It may also be helpful for you to realize that a certain amount of confusion and indecision is to be expected. These five questions may help you think about whether a topic is appropriate:

1. Will the topic hold your interest for several weeks or months?
2. Is the topic something about which you already know but can build upon or extend?
3. Does the topic fit the requirements of the assignment?
4. Is sufficient information available on the topic?
5. Do you have adequate time and resources to investigate the topic?

Your mission is to think of possible topics, consider the probable outcome of each, weigh the prospects, and choose one to research.

After deciding on your topic, it is important not to rush or unduly pressure yourself to "dig right in." It takes time for thoughts to develop to the point where you can make an intelligent decision about the research topic. Slow down and consider the topic; think clearly. Again, there are basic steps with regard to locating ideas or topics:

- *Read.* Real writers read a lot—broadly about a variety of areas. This does not merely mean textbooks . . . or books. Reading scholarly newspapers, magazines, journals, and so forth, are excellent sources to broaden your thoughts and ideas.
- *Look for problems, not answers.* When reading, seek out questions and unresolved issues. Take a fresh look at an old issue. Write by posing interesting questions and ideas.
- *Record your ideas.* If you don't keep track of what you are thinking, you will most likely forget it. The format for recording your thoughts is not important as long as it works for you.
- *Ask people.* Asking questions is not an indication of ignorance; it shows interest, concern, and the desire to learn. You can learn much from the experience, wisdom, and ideas of others.

Exercise 2.1: Determining a Topic

A. Your teacher has given you the broad subject of "gambling." You are to list 10 possible topics relating to this subject (for example, gambling and addiction). List your 10 topics below:

1.
2.
3.
4.
5.
6.
7.
8.
9.
10.

Where did you discover these topics? (for example, using search words on the Internet or visiting the library and so forth).

B. Your instructor has asked you to write a research paper on any topic concerning public schools in America today.
What topic did you come up with? _____
Describe, specifically, the process of choosing your topic. _____
_____
_____

GETTING STARTED

Locating Information about Your Topic

You have selected your topic and you are ready to learn more about it. Information concerning your topic may be found in books, print and online periodicals, print and online newspapers, the Internet, listservs, e-mails; by talking to others; and in a variety of other possible sources. Your choice of sources will depend on your research. For instance, if you are looking for tomorrow's weather, you might consult a local newspaper; if you are looking for a good movie to see, you could consult a friend; if you are looking for information on a country in the Middle East, you may perhaps consult a book, print or online journal, newspaper, or the Internet.

Learning to Focus

Once you have selected your topic, the next process is to explore information about the general topic in search of a *focus* for your research. A focus may be one aspect of the general topic on which you choose to concentrate, or it may be a central theme within the topic. Forming a focus for research marks a turning point in the research process. Before you form a focus, you gather general information on your topic. After you decide on a focus, you gather specific information about your area of focus. The way to do this is to explore several possible choices and decide on one that appears to promise the most success. The focus of the topic should be an aspect that you find particularly interesting and thought provoking. It should motivate you and encourage you to gather and form ideas and opinions about the topic. This is not necessary when you *want* to research cars, for example, because you are preparing to purchase a new one. Here, the motivation is "built-in," but when you are doing a project for class, the key is to find a way to make it relevant to your own life.

There may be more than one direction in which you can go while developing your topic—each of these possibilities needs to be explored. Library resources to identify and focus your topic are vital to your research success. Remember, however, that different sources of information may present opposing or conflicting views that seem unconnected and inconsistent. You must identify a unifying thread or theme for your research. Exploring many possible choices forms a focus, and deciding on the specific focus will determine the direction your research will take. All of this is critical before proceeding with your information collection. Although a definite focus should be formed at this point in the research process, the focus need not remain static; it may continue to take shape as long as the research continues. Before the focus is formed, it is normal to feel confused, lost, and even worried; after the focus has been formed, you will probably feel relieved. You will have determined your goal, and you will have a greater sense of direction.

The following may also be helpful when focusing your research

- What exactly is your topic? (Write it down.)
- What aspects of your topics are you interested in? (Write them down.)

- Think of keywords, synonyms, and other ways to express your topic; also consider opposite terms. (Write them down.)
- How current does the information need to be?
- How will you use the information?
- What types of formats do you want to use (charts, graphs, tables, short articles, long articles, news stories, photos, illustrations, scholarly articles, books, videos, bibliographies, and so forth)?

For additional ideas about selecting a topic, view "Further Reading" and the "Webliography" at the end of this chapter.

Thesis Statement

A *thesis statement* is helpful for keeping you on track. It is the point you are going to discuss or prove in your paper—or in real-life situations. A thesis statement should act as mortar—holding together the various elements of a paper (or your idea), summarizing the main point, and guiding the paper's (or your idea's) development. A thesis statement is an assertion, not a statement of fact, and often will be expressed in a sentence or two. Thesis statements take a stand, for example:

- Female students learn better in all-women colleges.
- The death penalty should be abolished.
- Televised news stories about suicide trigger a significant increase in the teen suicide rate.
- Near-death experiences signify that an afterlife exists.
- Teenage gang activity can only be stopped with early education in the public school systems.

A thesis is the main idea, not the title. It is narrow, not broad; specific, not general. A good thesis statement has one main point rather than several and typically features four attributes:

1. It addresses a subject about which people could reasonably disagree.
2. It deals with a subject that can be researched and described.
3. It expresses one main idea.
4. It asserts your conclusions about a subject.

Collecting Information

The next task is that of collecting information. This task should be approached in a systematic, organized manner. You must become proficient in identifying, reading, and taking notes about the information you locate.

If your research is to be effective, you must make a series of crucial choices as you begin to collect information. First, it is important to consult a variety of resources. Each type of resource (for example, a book or a journal) has its own attributes. These attributes are discussed in the next paragraph. Second, it is vital that you evaluate the information collected for accuracy and authority, bias, currency, and scope.

The most familiar information sources are books, journals, magazines, and newspapers. Books cover virtually every imaginable topic. Today books come in two formats: print and electronic. Journals (or magazines/periodicals) also come in both print and electronic formats (some are full-text, others merely abstracts). Journals are a good source for scholarly information, both current and historical. Often editorial policy requires that other experts review journal articles for accuracy, writing style, and so forth (referred to as "peer-reviewed journals"). Magazines are less academic. They typically contain popular-culture issues, leisure reading, hobbies, and so on. Newspapers cover local, national, and worldwide current events, as well a variety of other topics.

Today, much information is retrieved from the Internet, an unorganized medium that varies greatly in quality. Enormous amounts of information from Web sites, electronic journals, newspapers, and electronic books are available on the Internet—but not all of it is truthful, accurate, authoritative, current, or reliable. Because the Internet lacks organization, it can be quite difficult to locate the information you are seeking efficiently and effectively. All Internet (and other) information should be closely evaluated. Practice collecting information using Exercise 2.2.

Exercise 2.2: Collecting Information

Select a topic of interest to you. Write it down:_____.
Locate 10 information sources for this topic. Write them below:

Type of Source   Name of Source   Author or Creator

1.
2.
3.
4.
5.
6.
7.
8.
9.
10.

Why did you select these particular sources for your chosen topic?
Again, it is critical that you search a wide variety of resources and that you always evaluate each source you locate for accuracy and authority, bias, currency, and scope. Collecting information is a vital step in the research process. One cannot locate an answer or draw a conclusion without a wide variety of appropriate and accurate resources. Become familiar with resources—books, journals, reference materials, electronic sources, online databases and indexes, the Internet, people, and so forth.

Organize Your Research

As anyone who has begun a Google search only to be confronted with literally millions of results knows, simply finding raw information and doing research are too very different activities. No matter how much material you find, it will be of little use to you unless you can think about it within an organizational framework. Doing research is not simply about finding answers, it is about making meaning, shaping solutions to immediate problems from the available information. Such an effect can never be achieved unless your thinking is well structured from the outset. The four research models described in the previous chapter should be helpful in this regard, though it is important that you try to find the system that works best for you. Regardless of the approach you take, there are a few basic research steps to assist you as work toward completing a project.

1. *Identify and develop your topic.* Topic identification and development requires basic research of the idea you are considering.
2. *Locate background information.* Read about your topic. If you are conducting Internet research, look up keywords and then synonyms of those keywords to narrow your search. It takes time to find just what you want. Remember, textbooks and other print sources are also useful for integrating information into your topic. (This will be further explored in Chapters 3 and 5.)
3. *Use the library.* Online databases and indexes are extremely helpful for locating recent articles on your topic. Learn how to access and use these databases and indexes appropriately. Remember, some online articles contain only abstracts (you must locate the journal), and some are full-text. (Chapter 4 will explain this in more detail.)
4. *Locate information on the Internet.* This is not always easy. Use search engines, subject directories, and the Invisible (or Deep) Web to locate materials efficiently on the Internet. (See Chapter 5.)
5. *Look for information in other formats.* Consider videotapes, CD-ROMs, DVDs, and audiotapes. These, too, are valuable for your research.
6. *Remember to evaluate everything you locate.* See Chapter 6 regarding how to evaluate information. It is a critical component of effective research.
7. *Cite what you find and where you found it.* In other words, write down where you located the information and all of the accompanying information (title, author, place of publication, publisher, publication date, which are all required information for the bibliography). (See Chapter 8 for citation styles and sources.)
8. *Work from the general to the specific.* Locate background information first, and then use more specific and recent resources.
9. *Do not forget the obvious tools* Use dictionaries and thesauri to assist you.

(The above can be printed out from the companion Web site.)

Exercise 2.3: Organized Research

- Identify a topic of interest to you. Write it down:_____.
  Locate three sources of background information. List them below:
  - TYPE of Source   NAME of Source

  1.
  2.
  3.

- Locate three full-text, online database articles concerning your topic. List them below:
  - Name of JOURNAL   Name of ARTICLE

  1.
  2.
  3.

- Identify a total of ten Web pages found from a variety of search engines. List them below:
  - TYPE   URL

  1.
  2.
  3.
  4.
  5.
  6.
  7.
  8.
  9.
  10.

- Identify five sources that are neither print nor the Internet (for example, videotapes) concerning your topic. List them below:
  - TYPE of Source   TITLE of Source

  1.
  2.
  3.
  4.
  5.

CONCLUSION

Learning the process of seeking information is as important as expanding your understanding of subject matter. Ideas lead to the need for further information, and this continues until the search is concluded. The process of information gathering can lead to your becoming information literate and creating a successful research project. You must become conscious of your own thoughts and feelings as you progress through the research process. You will eventually become aware of how to systematically work though the stages of research and information-access/literacy—lifelong learning. Remember that it is critical to consult a variety of resources before deciding on your precise research topic. You should not be solely dependent on one or two sources. It is also important to evaluate the information you locate. There is no doubt that there is an enormous amount of information from which to choose. Selecting and locating a research topic, along with finding a focus, creating a thesis statement, collecting appropriate information from a wide variety of sources (and evaluating them), and "good writing" are your first large steps in creating effective and relevant research.

REFERENCES AND FURTHER READING

Bazeley, Michael. 2004. "There Are Web Sites to Try When Search Engines Fail." *Knight Rider Tribune Business News Washington,* May 19.

Byerly, Greg. 2004. "The ABCs of Grammar, Spelling and Writing." *School Library Media Activities Monthly,* 20: 7.

Haycock, Ken. 2004. "Kids Search Tools: The Best for Grade 4–10." *Teacher-Librarian,* 31: 4.

Haycock, Ken, Michelle Dober, and Barbara Edwards. 2003. *Neal-Schuman Authoritative Guide to Kids' Search Engines, Subject Directories, and Portals.* New York: Neal-Schuman.

Junion-Metz, Gail. 2004. "Footnotes for the Confused." *School Library Journal,* 50: 8.

Medford, Randolph Hock. 2004. *Click Everywhere: The Extreme Searcher's Internet Handbook: A Guide for the Serious Searcher.* Toronto, Canada: CyberAge Books.

Milam, Peggy. 2002. *InfoQuest: A New Twist on Information Literacy.* Worthington, OH: Linworth.

Montante, Sarah. 2004. "Good Writers Weren't Born That Way." *Literacy Cavalcade,* 56: 7.

Montante, Sarah. 2005. "Writing the Research Paper." *Literacy Cavalcade,* 57: 6.

O'Donnell, Carol Porter. 2004. "Beyond the Yellow Highlighter: Teaching Annotation Skills to Improve Reading Comprehension." *English Journal,* 93: 5.

Pappas, Marjorie L. 2003. "Writing Editorials." *School Library Media Activities Monthly*, 19: 10.

Schlein, Alan M. 2002. *Find It Online: The Complete Guide to Online Research* (3rd ed.). Tempe, AZ: Facts on Demand Press.

Strickland, James. 2004. "Just the FAQs: An Alternative to Teaching the Research Paper." *English Journal*, 94: 1.

Weinberg, Steve. 2005. "Writers Discuss Style, Voice, and What Makes for Good Writing." *Writer*, 118: 2.

Whitley, Peggy, Catherine Olson, and Susan Goodwin. 2001. *99 Jumpstarts to Research*. Greenwood Village, CO: Libraries Unlimited.

WEBLIOGRAPHY

Basic Online Spelling and Vocabulary Resources

Merriam-Webster Dictionary
http://m-w.com
The Merriam-Webster, Inc. online dictionary.
Merriam-Webster's Word Central
www.wordcentral.com
This is an interesting Web site for students to learn words, grammar, etc.
Thesaurus.com
www.thesaurus.com
This site includes areas such as Reference.com, Translator, Dictionary.com, Feature Articles, and so forth.
Good Writing
EditAvenue.com
www.editavenue.com
This site offers a variety of editing services for a fee.
The Elements of Style
www.bartleby.com/141
This Web site provides, in a brief space, the principal requirements of plain English style.
Elements of Style
www.diku.dk/hjemmesider/studerende/myth/EOS/
This site, by William Strunk, Jr. includes subtitles such as "Elementary Rules of Usage, Principles of Composition."
Eleven Rules of Writing
http://junketstudies.com/rulesofw/
This site is a concise guide to some of the most commonly violated rules of writing, grammar, and punctuation.
The Nuts and Bolts of College Writing
http://nutsandbolts.washcoll.edu
This site addresses thinking, style, structure, mechanics, and so forth.

University of Wisconsin Writing Center: Grammar and Punctuation
www.wisc.edu/writetest/Handbook/GramPunct.html
This Web site includes areas such as: "How to Proofread," "Using Semicolons," "Using Dashes."

UW-Madison Writing Center: Stages of the Writing Process
www.wisc.edu/writetest/Handbook/Process.html
This Web site covers topics such as "Planning to Write," "Creating an Argument," "Working with Sources."

University of Wisconsin Center: Writer's Handbook
www.wisc.edu/writetest/Handbook
This site includes information such as "Stages of the Writing Process," "Grammar and Punctuation," and "Improving Your Writing Style."

Writing in Plain Language Using Plain English
www.ziskadesigns.co.uk/masterplain.html
This Web site addresses areas such as shorter sentences, words to avoid, clear layout, use of space.

Writing for Research

A+ Research and Writing
www.ipl.org/div/teen/aplus
This Web site was created specifically for teens learning to research and write.

The OWL Family of Sites
http://owl.english.purdue.edu
This is a series of sites that offer online writing, research, and MLA and APA style help. Particularly helpful is the OWL Writing Lab.

Chapter 3

How Do I Find the Information I Need?

INTRODUCTION

While there are volumes of information about virtually every topic imaginable, it often seems difficult to find what we are looking for when we need it most. If we hope to consistently track down what we are looking for, we need to learn the art of searching. To go about searching properly you need to make the right choices, figuring out what to look at, what questions to ask, and when to ask them. You will have to learn to consider things like the time frame of your searching and the appropriate resources for a given topic. For example, if you want to locate scholarly information regarding the hurricanes and tornadoes of 2005, you would search online databases and subject directories. Searching requires careful planning and thoughtful preparation. In this chapter we will consider some of the means you can employ to make your searching as effective as possible.

PLANNING YOUR SEARCH

A Possible Search Plan

A search of any kind requires a confluence of factors if it is to be successful. Among other things, it calls for a high degree of interest, a lot of curiosity, and a willingness to spend some time looking for the best information available. Research is a journey, and just as you would not expect a car trip to end the moment you put your hands on the steering wheel, you should anticipate long and sometimes bumpy roads while on the way to the information you desire. Fortunately, in the same way that a good map helps a trip go more smoothly, a search plan helps ease your searches. Here is a sample plan:

- *Step One: Understand your research assignment topic.* If it is not clear to you ask your instructor, make sure you know exactly what you're looking for before you begin. View some general resources about your topic to gain a better understanding of the area (for example, encyclopedias, dictionaries, handbooks, directories, etc.).
- *Step Two: Create your search plan.* You need a search plan to begin your search for information. Your search plan should consist of keywords that describe the information you are seeking, along with information about the relationship between the keywords. From your assignment topic, it is wise to develop at least two "concepts, or related ideas," of the topic along with keywords. For example, let's say that your assignment is to research some aspect of the Underground Railroad. Concept one could be about a major leader of the Underground Railroad, such as Harriet Tubman. Possible keywords might include: Harriet Tubman, Underground Railroads, slavery, emancipation, Civil War, and so on. Concept two might consider what role the Quakers played in the Underground Railroads. Possible keywords may include Quakers, slaves, abolitionists, and so forth. By compiling a list of similar and related terms (synonyms—use a thesaurus to look for these), your chances of locating relevant information will greatly increase. To assist you with this step make use of the following figure:

Observe and complete Figure 3.1.

		Please write a sentence describing your topic		
1	Search Question			
		List as many as needed		
2	Major Concepts	1. 2. 3.		
		Search Terms		
3	Concepts 1	Concepts 2		Concepts 3
or				
or				
or				
or				
or				
or				
or				
or				
or				

Figure 3.1   Search Strategy

- *Step Three: Decide on the types and formats of information sources you might need for your assignment.* You should select the types and formats of information sources that best meet the needs of the assignment.
    - o Information types might include
        - historical
        - current
        - government
        - technical
        - statistical
        - research
        - legal
        - demographic
    - o Information formats might include:
        - books (print and electronic)
        - journal articles (print and electronic)
        - videos
        - charts

- CD-ROMs
- DVDs
- newspapers
- information located on Web sites, etc.
- people (interviews)

Information is typically created in response to an event or phenomena and is published in several different forms and sources. The different types of information sources created sometimes depend on how much time has elapsed between the event and the creation of publications about the event. For example, consider the Underground Railroad assignment. Ponder the time period of the Underground Railroad; let's say the mid-nineteenth century. From this information, you may determine that much of the information you need might come from print sources (because it is not a current topic), such as books, encyclopedias (print, CD-ROM, or online), videotapes, and perhaps some electronic or print journal articles and the Internet (however, these resources are less likely to include information necessary for the assignment).

- *Step Four: Get ready to search by creating search statements.* A search statement is a set of instructions or a group of keywords that will assist you in locating appropriate information. For instance (once again using the Underground Railroad assignment), possible search statements might be "Harriet Tubman and Underground Railroad" or "Quakers and slavery" or "abolitionists and the Underground Railroad."
- *Step Five: Locate and obtain the information needed for your assignment.* Identify the type of reference—a book, book chapter, video, journal article, and so on. Always write down the name, location, and all other pertinent data about the resource for use as a possible reference in your research paper. *Step Six: Evaluate the information/resources you have gathered.* (Refer to Chapter 6 for detailed information regarding evaluation of print, nonprint, and electronic resources. This chapter includes four criteria for evaluating information: accuracy and authority, objectivity, currency, and scope.)

Exercise 3.1: Search Plan

Your teacher has assigned you the research project "Home Schooling: Should It Be Allowed?" Please complete the information below regarding this topic.

1. *List the types and formats of information sources you might need for your assignment.*
2. *Create and write down a minimum of two search statements.*
3. *Make a list of possible resources for this assignment.*

A CLOSER LOOK AT SEARCH TOOLS

Finally, let's take a look at some possible resources in more depth:

- Books: Books are typically in print format, although more and more electronic (e-text) volumes are becoming available. For the most part, reference and textbooks are written by experts and evaluated by a number of authoritative individuals before publication. Therefore, the information is typically accurate and reliable. Remember, however, that some books, such as trade books, contain false, biased, inaccurate information. In addition, generally speaking, books can become dated very quickly, particularly in areas such as medicine, technology, and geography. There exists a wide variety of reference books that are excellent for conducting research, ranging from atlases to handbooks to directories to dictionaries, and many others. Reference books are a good starting point to locate facts about a particular topic. Books are useful; however, a combination of search tools provides the most accurate and complete information.
- Academic Journals: Journals are also typically written and reviewed by scholars. The information is usually accurate and can be extremely current. Scholarly articles are viewed as having credibility and authority. There is a wide a variety of journals available on every imaginable subject. Many journals can be accessed electronically via online databases (such as ProQuest, EBSCO, etc.). These online databases allow you to access numerous articles from a variety of journals magazines, and newspapers. Some databases con-

tain full-text articles and some merely provide abstracts. Some of the databases containing full-text articles include Academic Search Elite, Business Source Premier, and ScienceDirect.

- Magazines: Magazines are not *generally* considered scholarly, although some specialized magazines include scholarly information. Many magazines cover popular culture and leisure concerns. Magazines include a wide variety of topics; a few examples are *Golf Digest, Popular Mechanics, Computer World, Road and Track, Ladies Home Journal,* and *Billboard.* The targeted audience of many magazines is the general public. In addition, as with journals, some are now in electronic format (e-journal or e-zine).

- Newspapers: Depending on their focus, newspapers cover local, national, and worldwide current events as well as a variety of other subjects. Some newspapers are specific to a particular topic, such as the *Wall Street Journal,* which is a newspaper covering news about the stock market. Many newspapers are published daily and, therefore, are extremely current. A large number of newspapers can now be accessed electronically.

- Library Catalogs: Library catalogs are a record of all of the materials that a particular library owns. They are organized and easily searchable. Most library catalogs are automated (electronic, called Online Public Access Catalogs or OPACs) **and** use keyword searching. (In keyword searching, the database software searches for the occurrence of the search term in one or more fields of each record, such as in the title or abstract). Many library catalogs can be accessed from locations other than the library, for example, from your home or office.

- Periodical Databases: Periodical databases provide a searchable index to magazine, journal, and newspaper articles. A periodical is any information that is issued regularly, for example, daily, weekly, monthly, annually. Again, examples of electronic databases are ProQuest, EBSCO, CINAHL (Note: Periodical databases are similar to "journal databases." They provide numerous articles from a variety of journals, magazines, and newspapers—either abstracts or full-text articles.)

Exercise 3.2: Online Periodical Databases

Please view the following:
How to Interpret a Record in an Index or Database
www.ithaca.edu/library/course/periodindex.html

For this exercise, locate any online periodical database (Infotrac, EBSCO, PsycINFO, ProQuest, PubMed, etc.). Look for articles about a specific topic that were written between July 2004 and now; only select and read full-text articles. Print out your findings and share them with your instructor and classmates. Were you pleased or displeased with the number of articles. If you were displeased, what could you do to broaden the number?

Exercise 3.3: Searching

Try your hand at the "search plan" explained in this chapter. Think of an area of interest to you (for example, Afghanistan, dyslexia, car racing, women in politics, etc.) and complete Figure 3.2, *which can be printed from the companion Web site*. Sometimes, writing it down or "putting it in black-and-white" is helpful. When ideas move from your mind to the page, they become more real and you remain more focused. That is why it is recommended to write it on a worksheet. Remember, effective searching begins with effective search strategies, which begin with clear and interesting questions. You may need to refer back to this chapter for assistance . . . but this procedure should soon become easier and easier.

STEPS	TASK	DESCRIPTION
1	Write down a specific description of your research assignment.	
2	Visit the library and view 3 general resources about your assignment/topic.	1. 2. 3.
3	Write 5 keywords (remember to use a thesaurus).	1. 2. 3. 4. 5.
4	Develop 2 Concepts of the topic.	1. 2.
5	List the types and formats of materials you might need for your research.	
6	Create 2 search statements.	1. 2.
7	Locate resources (print, nonprint, online, people) appropriate for your research.	1. 2 3. 4. 5.
8	Write down pertinent information about each of the 5 resources (where found, title, author or creator, publication date, place of publication, publisher, summary).	1. 2. 3. 4. 5.
9	Evaluate the 5 resources (refer to Chapter 6).	

Figure 3.2   Planning a Search

SEARCH TOOLS AND TECHNIQUES

Effective search tools and techniques are critical to successful research. Consider this scenario: All of the books, magazines, journals, and newspapers in your library (or home) are piled in a big heap on the floor. How would you find the specific information you need? Tough, huh? Luckily, people have developed techniques and tools to make searching much easier for you. When using an electronic library catalog, you can search for materials by author, title, subject, and so on—a wide variety of methods of sorting through the resources. However, there are more advanced search strategies that can assist you in locating information even more easily. Let's take a closer look at a variety of these search tools and techniques:

- Boolean Logic: George Boole originally developed this approach in the mid–1800s. It allows you to refine your search by using the connector words AND, OR, and NOT. These words can help you limit or broaden your search. Using AND or NOT between keywords will reduce the number of results found (however, they reduce results in different ways). For example, "Quakers AND Underground Railroad" will locate resources that could contain both of the terms, "Quakers" and "Underground Railroad." "Quakers NOT Underground Railroad" will not locate information on the Underground Railroad as it relates to Quakers, but it will find materials on Quakers. Always remember that there is a possible loss of good information when using the Boolean Operator NOT. Using OR between keywords will increase the number of results found. OR is best used with topics that do not retrieve many results. "Quakers OR Underground Railroad" will find resources that contain either the term Quakers or the term Underground Railroad. See Figure 3.3 for a visual representation of Boolean Logic.

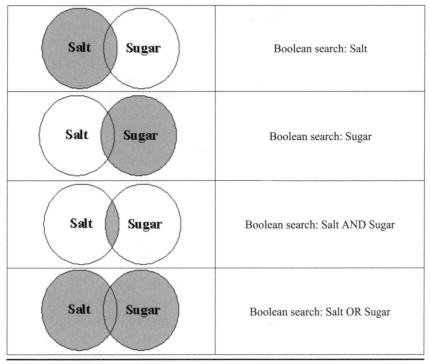

Figure 3.3   Boolean Logic Venn Diagram

- Limiters: Limiters can assist you to focus your topic and decrease the number of results that you will need to read. Limiters include such items as material type, language, date published and so forth. In other words, when conducting a search, you can "select" the type "video" and the information requested will be listed in that format only. Another example is date published. You may select, for example, the year "2004." This will limit your retrievals to information written only in the year 2004.
- Truncation: Truncation is helpful when searching for terms that could have several endings. An example of this search strategy is to type educat*. By doing so, you will be allowed to find information on education, educator, educate, and other terms that begin with "educate."
- Phrase Searching: This tool utilizes quotation marks to search for results that contain those words together rather than search for all instances of each separate word. The phrase "sexually transmitted

diseases" is an example. This phrase will locate information regarding diseases that are transmitted sexually.

- Wildcards: Wildcards can be helpful when you are unsure of the correct spelling of a word. A wildcard is the insertion of a question mark in place of a letter that you do not know. For example, lab?r will locate both the U.S. and British spellings of labor/labour. Another example is wom?n, which will capture irregular singular and plurals of woman. Wildcards are sometimes called internal truncation, or stemming.

- Match-All Search: This technique is similar to the Boolean tool "AND." This is a search for pages containing all of your search terms that uses the symbol "+." For example, "Quakers + Underground Railroad" will provide information that pertains to both terms, Quakers and Underground Railroad. Likewise, you may use the symbol "-" like the Boolean operator, NOT. "Quakers – Underground Railroad" will not locate information on the Underground Railroad as it relates to Quakers, but will find materials on Quakers.

- Title Searching: Many of the major search engines and databases allow you to search with the HTML title of a Web page. This is the text that appears within the title page of a document. For example, a page may have an HTML title like this: <title>Harriet Tubman and the Underground Railroad<title>. By using this, you will proceed directly to that Web site or database. If you know the Web site or database's title, you can use this method of searching.

Exercise 3.4: Search Terms

Now, let's see if you understand all of this newly acquired information. Take the short multiple-choice quiz below to test your knowledge.

What are Boolean operators?

1. The programming language that allows you to display your
    search results.
2. The terms "AND" "OR" and "NOT" that are used to create
    search expressions.
3. The terms "WITHIN" and "NEAR" used for locating nearby
    terms in your search.

Which search expression will return the largest number of results?

1. Movies AND Harrison Ford
2. Movies OR Harrison Ford
3. Movies AND Harrison Ford AND Tom Hanks
4. Movies OR Harrison Ford NOT Tom Hanks

Which of the following is an example of truncation?

1. listen*
2. locat*
3. fin*
4. Hank*

Which of the following is a wildcard?

1. can?t
2. lilly?
3. m?n
4. m*n

A limiter does which of the following to your search?

1. Broadens your search
2. Narrows your search
3. Eliminates your search

Certain symbols are used in place of the Boolean operators. They are

1. ? and !
2. + and −
3. (and)
4. " and "

By exploring search engines, you can determine which tools and techniques are specific to a particular one (for example, Google, AltaVista, HotBot, etc.). The more experienced you become with effectively and efficiently using search tools and techniques and the more familiar you become with a variety of search engines, the easier your research will become. Keep these three tips in mind while you are searching for information:

Tip 1:   Your search results ("hits"):
o Do they match up with the search terms you used?
o Do you need to use different search terms for this database?
o Do the references match the keywords but not the kind of information you need?
o Did you enter the search statement correctly and use the correct commands?
o Are you in the most appropriate database?

Tip 2:   If you received too many references, you can
o add another concept to make it more specific (narrow your search).
o make certain that you are using the Boolean operators correctly.
o add limits to your search (for example, document type or particular years).

Tip 3:   If your search didn't yield enough references:
o try searching a broader term.
o make certain that you are using the Boolean operators correctly.
o use alternative keywords (synonyms).
o truncate search terms if needed.
o try another database.

Exercise 3.5: Subject Directories

Subject directories, such as Yahoo, depend on humans for their listings. Humans collect and read Web pages and decide what categories to list them under. You can then browse through the categories to find lists of relevant Web sites. Often a search button is included to help you find which categories your topic is listed under. The total scope of a directory like Yahoo is much smaller than that of a search engine, but your search results are often much more relevant than with search engines.

Use the subject directory Yahoo to browse for a topic of your choosing.

Explain the procedures you went through and any useful tips you may have encountered while browsing the Yahoo directory.

CONCLUSION

Knowing about various search tools and search techniques is critical to effective research. Awareness and use of these can make searching much more efficient and accurate. Always begin by searching a number of sources (books, online journals, etc.) and continue by using the previously mentioned techniques and tools to locate the precise information you need for your research project.

REFERENCES AND FURTHER READING

Balas, Janet L. 2004. "The Way You Organize Your Electronic Resources Really Matters." *Computers in Libraries,* 24 (1): 36–39.

Bazeley, Michael. 2004. "There Are Web Sites to Try When Search Engines Fail." *Knight Ridder Tribune Business News,* May 19.

Doe, Charles G. 2005. "A look at . . . Subscription Web Sites." *Multimedia & Internet@Schools,* 12 (1): 7–11.

Gogolski, Adam. 2004. "Deciding When to Use Which Search Resource." *Inside the Internet Louisville,* 11: 8.

Haycock, Ken, and Michelle Dober, and Barbara Edwards. 2004. *Neal-Schuman Authoritative Guide to Kids' Search Engines, Subject Directories, and Portals.* New York: Neal-Schuman.

Medford, Randolph Hock. 2004. *Click Everywhere: The Extreme Searcher's Internet Handbook: A Guide for the Serious Searcher.* Toronto, Canada: Cyberage Books.

Powell, William. 2002. "Bully Boolean." *Training and Development* 56: 21–22.

Reutter, Vicki. 2005. "Research Skills for Students (Series)." *School Library Journal,* 51 (2): 69–70.

Schlein, Alan M. 2002. *Find It Online: The Complete Guide to Online Reseaarch.* Tempe, AZ: Facts on Demand Press.

Strickland, James. 2004. "Just the FAQs: An Alternative to Teaching the Research Paper. *English Journal,* 94 (1): 23–28.

WEBLIOGRAPHY

Boolean Searching on the Internet
http://library.albany.edu/internet/boolean.html
This Web site is an easy-to-read and comprehensive guide to Boolean searching on Internet search engines.

Critically Analyzing Information Sources
www.library.cornell.edu/okuref/research/skill26.htm
This site covers initial appraisal and content analysis; this is very useful.

Finding Information on the Web
http://library.austincc.edu/help/srching/srching.htm
This Web site discusses "Search Engines," "Searching Techniques" (keywords, truncation and Boolean Operators), and finding a place to start.

The 5 Most Common Search Engine Mistakes
www.darwinmag.com/read/090103/search.html
This Web site includes a consolidated list of things you most definitely do not want to be doing if you want a high ranking in the search engines; this is quite interesting.

How Boolean Logic Works
www.howstuffworks.com/boolean1.htm
This Web site provides additional information regarding Boolean searching.

Information Skills
www.fno.org/libskill.html
This site discusses questioning, planning, gathering, sorting, synthesizing, evaluating and reporting information.

Internet Search Tools—Quick Reference Guide
www.itrc.ucf.edu/conferences/pres/srchtool.html
This is an extremely useful Web site that explains when to use which search engine, subject directory, etc.

Learning to Research on the Web
www.ipl.org/div/teen/aplus/internet.htm
This site includes information such as understanding how search engines work, learning the difference between a search engine and a directory, learning essential browser skills.

OWL: Searching the World Wide Web
http://owl.english.purdue.edu/handouts/research/r_websearch2.html
This Web site discusses kinds of search engines, using search engines, using Boolean operators, and much more.

Skills for Online Searching
www.ipl.org/div/teen/aplus/skills.htm
This useful Web site covers items such as the following: learning how search syntax works, Boolean Logic, wildcards, truncation, and phrase searching.

WebWizard: Your Guide to Becoming an Effective Web Searcher
www.bgsu.edu/colleges/library/infosrv/lue/webwizard/searching.html
This is an excellent Web site on searching the World Wide Web, including, "What is the best search engine?" "How Do You Use Boolean Operators?" and "What Are Some Common Obstacles?"

Which Search Engine?
http://library.queensu.ca/inforef/instruct/search.htm
This Web site discusses search engines and subject directories. Many links are provided; it is a good Web site.

Working the Web for Education
http://ozline.com/learning/theory.html
This Web site covers "Theory and Practice on Integrating the Web for Learning."

Chapter 4

How Can the Library
(and Virtual Library) Help Me?

INTRODUCTION

While there are a great many ways to track down information, there are few better places to begin a search than a library. Libraries come in many forms, but their function is always to index and make available large amounts of information. Though famous as storehouses for books, libraries also often carry a wide variety of different resources in a plethora of formats and media. What a library carries is dependent on the community it serves—academic libraries on university campuses tend to have more scholarly collections than conventional public libraries, for example. Accordingly, it is important to know what you are looking for before you set out to a library. Libraries of all types, however, are exceptional jumping-off points for research of any kind. When you start from a library, there is almost no limit to the directions you can travel.

A relatively new development is the virtual library. These are online indexes that make available virtual books, articles, and other information in an electronic form. The best virtual libraries, some of which are discussed in this chapter, are often just as thorough and well organized as libraries in the real world.

Understanding libraries of all kinds is a crucial part of developing information literacy. Accordingly, this chapter will cover some crucial information about the values and ideals embodied and championed by libraries. It will also discuss some strategies for making use of library resources online.

LIBRARY POLICIES AND SERVICES

It is common for a library's mission statement to read something like this: The library will provide comprehensive information services to meet the curricular, research, cultural, and recreational needs of all users. This mission will be accomplished by providing

- a rich variety of print, nonprint, and electronic materials and re-sources that enhance the curriculum as well as additional resources for personal improvement and recreation.
- assistance and instruction in the use of information resources by a staff of trained professionals.
- a learning environment with services and equipment that facilitate the use of materials and resources.

In order to meet these requirements libraries must write and uphold certain policies and procedures. These are critical documents to help assure that libraries can operate efficiently and effectively. They are also written to protect and assist all library users. Typically, policies are de-fined as "why" documents, and provide a rationale for doing something. On the other hand, procedures tell you "how" to do something.

Libraries have policies for areas such as circulation, access require-ments, and Internet use. These policies and procedures are for *your* ben-efit. They allow you such luxuries as freedom and access to appropriate, accurate, and current materials and equipment.

For an example of an academic library homepage, please explore

- Saint Leo University Online Library
  www.saintleo.edu/library

OR for an example of a public library homepage, please explore

- Louisville Free Public Library
  www.lfpl.org

Notice the "Ask-A-Librarian" section on the academic library site. It allows you to pose reference questions via the Internet—a big help, right? Notice, too, that the online library provides "Search for Articles and Abstracts," "Help Pages," and so forth. The public library Web site also offers a wealth of information, such as Research Tools, Ask-A-Librarian (like above), Reader's Corner, Kids and Teen Programs, Meet the Authors Month, 2006 Library Events, Computer classes, and much more.

Libraries provide a wide variety of services, depending on the type and size of the library. *Examples* of library services include

- *Reserve materials* (materials placed on reserve by an instructor for your specific use; typically held at the circulation desk or special reserve section in larger libraries).
- *Interlibrary loans* (acquisition of materials such as books or copies of journal articles not available at that particular library but borrowed from another library for your use).
- *Assistance* (personal, online, or both) with areas such as basic research, evaluation of resources, citing resources, writing/research tools, and reference services, to name a few. Librarians provide numerous reference services to library users. This extremely helpful service assists you in locating many types of information. Librarians can assist you with "quick" reference questions or more detailed and involved issues. You can ask reference questions in person, on the telephone, via e-mail, and even by chat reference—depending on the library and your personal preferences. Look around on your library's Web site or visit it in person to find out what services are available. It is to your benefit to utilize the services of the reference librarian!
- *"Online, real-time" reference services*, a relatively new service. Students and librarians "co-browse" the reference materials together. If you are attending school, check out what virtual reference services are available.

It may be useful at this point to review how to look for resources in the "traditional' library." Materials are arranged (or cataloged) such that you can locate them quickly and easily. Two major classification systems are used in libraries today: Library of Congress (LC) and Dewey Decimal Classification (DDC). Most small and school libraries use Dewey Decimal; most academic and larger public libraries use the Library of Congress Classification System. Regardless of the classification system employed, you can enter keywords (author, title, subject, etc.) into the online library computer to locate the appropriate book (arranged on the shelf by a "call number"). It is helpful to practice locating sources in your library using its classification system.

Exercise 4.1: How Libraries Work

It's good to understand "how libraries work." Libraries should become your best friends while conducting research. Libraries house organized, easy-to-access print and nonprint materials. They also have computers loaded with enormous amounts of information (indexes, databases, etc.) to make your research easier. In addition, they have "live" librarians, who can assist you with all of your research needs!

Do you know what rights you have as a library user? The next time you are in front of a computer, explore the following Web sites (produced by the American Library Association). You may learn something new and interesting!

"The American Library Association Library Bill of Rights"
- www.ala.org/work/freedom/lbr.html

    Did you know that according to the American Library Association, "materials should not be excluded because of the origin, background, or views of those contributing to their creation?"

"Code of Ethics of the American Library Association"
- www.ala.org/alaorg/oif/ethics.html

    Did you know that the American Library Association "upholds the principles of intellectual freedom and resists all efforts to censor library resources?"

"American Library Association Freedom of Information Act"
- www.ftrf.org/foia.html

    Did you know that the American Library Association claims that "censorship is harmful because it results in the opposite of true education and learning?"

"The Freedom to Read Statement"
- www.ala.org/alaorg/oif/freeread.html

    Did you know that "freedom to read is essential to our democracy . . . and it is continuously under attack?"

"Library of Congress Classification Outline"
- http://lcweb.loc.gov/catdir/cpso/lcco/lcco.html

    Did you know that the Library of Congress was first established as a legislative library in 1800?

These Web sites show the commitment of our libraries to the Library Bill of Rights, a free democracy and the freedom to learn as one chooses.

Library Online Assistance

Many libraries offer online assistance through the online library catalog, indexes, databases, and other Web links. A library's online public access catalog (OPAC) can typically be searched in a variety of methods: title keyword, author keyword, subject keyword, general keyword, series keyword, journal keyword, title browse, author browse, series browse, subject browse, journal browse, etc. This makes locating materials much more efficient and effective for you. As discussed in the last chapter, periodical indexes and databases allow you to search for citations to articles in popular magazines, scholarly journals, newspapers, dissertations, etc. Sometimes these databases have the complete, or full-text, articles; occasionally they contain only abstracts. These indexes and databases are often available both in the library and from remote locations, such as your home or a computer lab. Usually, to logon to the databases from outside of the library requires a combination of a special user identification (ID) and a password (available from that library or the academic institution to which it is attached). The following are *examples* of online indexes and databases that may be found in a library. Your library may have some of these or different ones not listed below. (Note: EBSCO, FirstSearch, ProQuest, etc., are database providers—they offer a variety of specific online databases.)

- Academic Search Premier (via EBSCO): Searches over 3,000 scholarly journals, magazines, and trade publications from all academic disciplines.
- AGRICOLA (via FirstSearch): Searches agriculture, forestry, and animal-science materials.
- Alt-Health Watch (via EBSCO): Provides articles on alternative approaches to health care and wellness.
- Alternative Press Index (via FirstSearch): Indexes approximately 300 journals covering cultural, economic, political, and social change.
- ArtAbstracts (via FirstSearch): Indexes articles from the world's leading arts and humanities journals.
- BioDigest (via FirstSearch): Provides life-science information in layperson terms.
- *Biography Index* (via FirstSearch): Contains full-text biography resources—articles, biographies, and Web sites.
- *Book Review Digest* (via FirstSearch): Provides abstracted reviews of fiction and nonfiction works.
- *BooksInPrint* (via FirstSearch): Provides information regarding in-print, out-of-print, and forthcoming books, with reviews.

- Business Source Elite (via EBSCO): Provides full text for over 1,000 business journals, magazines, and trade publications for news and events.
- Business Wire News (via EBSCO): A collection of full text newswires incorporating news from all over the world—information on business, political, economic and other diverse, international news events.
- *Chronicle of Higher Education* (via Chronicle): Provides a full coverage of the Chronicle of Higher Education.
- *CINAHL* (via FirstSearch): Contains a cumulated index of nursing and allied health literature.
- Consumers Index (via FirstSearch): Indexes numerous articles providing consumer information.
- DataTimes (via FirstSearch): Provides an index of United States, international and regional newspapers.
- *Dissertation Abstracts* (via FirstSearch): Contains abstracts of dissertations from all over the world.
- Education Abstracts (via FirstSearch): Includes leading publications in the field of education.
- *ERIC* (via FirstSearch): Contains abstracts of documents and journal articles on educational research and practice.
- FactSearch (via FirstSearch): Includes facts and statistics on topics of current interest.
- Facts.com (via Facts.com): Provides current-events information on the United States and world news in full text.
- GEOBASE (via FirstSearch): Contains worldwide literature on geography, geology, and ecology.
- *Government Printing Office* (via FirstSearch): Contains information concerning United States government publications.
- *Grove's Dictionary of Art Online* (via Groveart.com): This is the most comprehensive online reference resource for all aspects of the visual arts worldwide—prehistory to the present day, including articles, images, and Web sites relating to the visuals.
- Literature Resource Center (via Gale): Provides full-text resources with access to biographies, bibliographies, and critical essays of authors from every age and literary discipline.
- MEDLINE (via FirstSearch): Contains abstracted articles from several thousand medical journals.
- *Reader's Guide Abstracts* (via FirstSearch): Contains abstracts of articles from popular magazines.

- SIRS Government Reporter (via SIRS): Provides reports and information by and about the United States Government with full text.
- SIRS Renaissance (via SIRS): Contains information regarding arts and humanities with full text.
- SIRS Researcher (via SIRS): Provides articles on social, scientific, economic, and political issues worldwide.
- WilsonSelectPlus (via FirstSearch): Contains full text articles in science, humanities, education, and business.
- *WorldAlmanac* (via FirstSearch): Contains world facts and statistics.
- *WorldBook* (via FirstSearch): *The World Book Encyclopedia.*

Exercise 4.2: Indexes and Databases

Visit your local public, school, or academic library. This may take a bit of time, but it is well worth the effort! Each library purchases specific indexes and databases. The ones they buy depend on the size of the library, the type of library, and what the librarian selects. It is a good idea to talk to your librarian about the indexes and databases available in your library—and any other information you can acquire from him/her! Access a variety of the online indexes and databases that your library has available. What is the purpose of this task? Just as you learn more about riding a horse by doing it rather than reading about it, it is much easier to learn about indexes and databases if you explore and use them. Databases contain an enormous amount of information that may be useful for your research. Current journal and newspaper articles include relevant, specialized, and important information.

Each database serves a different purpose and population. For example, the *ERIC* database primarily locates information about education. The *CINAHL* database provides articles and abstracts that deal with nursing and health issues. The Literature Resource Center offers access to biographies, bibliographies, and critical analyses of authors from every age and literary discipline. NEWSBANK: America's Newspapers provides over 625 full-text U.S. newspapers. PsycINFO is valuable for psychology majors and researchers, while RIA Checkpoint is useful for tax issues, accounting, and corporate finance. Westlaw provides a collection of statutes, case-law materials, public records, and other legal resources; Wilson's Book Review Digest reviews current fiction and nonfiction materials and gives review excerpts and full-text reviews. By learning about various databases that your library holds, you can research more effectively and efficiently.

List the databases you accessed. What is their primary focus (area, subject)? Are they useful (contain lots of pertinent articles) and user friendly (easy to maneuver around in)? Which database did you rate the highest? Why?

VIRTUAL LIBRARIES

What are virtual libraries? Virtual libraries are directories that contain collections of resources that librarians or information specialists have carefully chosen and have organized in a logical way. The main difference between virtual libraries and directories is that virtual libraries are much smaller since the resources included are very carefully selected. The people who organize virtual libraries are typically on the lookout for three major types of information: subject guides, reference works, and specialized databases. Basically, virtual libraries provide databases, indexes, online library catalogs (from a variety of libraries), interlibrary loans, government information, and numerous services (including virtual reference desks)—all available online. A virtual libraries is a managed collection of information resources and services available electronically through the Internet. Many states now have their own online libraries; these are gateways for information and research assistance. Virtual libraries provide high-quality research and complex search services—they are organized information (libraries) through the Internet. However, it is important to understand that virtual libraries cannot perform *all* of the functions of an "actual library." Virtual libraries do not yet offer personal assistance, activities, or services for learning and enjoyment.

For additional information on virtual libraries, visit the following Web sites. (Also, contact your local library regarding your state's virtual library.)

- Education Virtual Library
  www.csu.edu.au/education/library.html
  This Web site provides information via a virtual university from Charles Sturt University (New South Wales, Australia).
- The WWW Virtual Library
  www.vlib.org
  This site includes areas to research from "agriculture" to "society." Note: numerous extremely specialized virtual libraries exist as well as general virtual libraries.
- ERAU Virtual Library
  www.embryriddle.edu/libraries/virtual
  This Web site is from the Embry-Riddle Aeronautical University (Daytona Beach, FL); it provides 1,911 links regarding aerospace and aviation.

Exercise 4.3: Virtual Libraries

Answer the following question using the Saint Leo University (Saint Leo, FL) online library (www.saintleo.edu/library). On the sidebar

- Click on "Research Guides." What print and online resources are available for the discipline, "criminal justice?"
- Click on "Media Services and Resources." How many video recordings about hurricanes are available?
- Click on "Library Information." For how long can a student check out a book?
- Click on "University Campus Library Resources." Does the Saint Leo University library offer Ask-A-Librarian? What is available through "LeoCat?" May a student at Saint Leo University check out a laptop computer?

CONCLUSION

As stated in the introduction of this chapter, it critical to remember that libraries offer structured access to practically everything about which you want to know and learn. Even with the rise of the Internet, libraries are more popular now than ever before. Whether traditional or virtual, libraries provide the answers to many of our questions; solutions for many of our problems. Become a friend with your librarian!

REFERENCES AND FURTHER READING

D'Angelo, Barbara J. 2001. "What Is a Virtual Library"? *Library Technology Reports* 37: 5–8.

Huff, James. 2003. "Defining the Non-Virtual Library." *American Libraries*, 34 (10): 36–37.

Junion-Metz, Gail. 2004. "Desperately Seeking Study Skills." *School Library Journal*, 50 (6): 30–31.

Mash, David S. 2003. "Libraries, Books and Academic Freedom." *Academe*, 89 (2): 50–55.

Reiner, Laura, and Allen Smith. 2003. "Digital Libraries." *Journal of Academic Librarianship*, 29: 1.

St. Lifer, Evan. 2005. "Guiding the Googlers." *School Library Journal*, 51 (1): 11–12.

Williams, Wilda W. 2002. "Planning for Library Services to People with Disabilities." *Library Journal* 127: 148–156.

WEBLIOGRAPHY

American Library Association

The American Library Association "Library Bill of Rights"
www.ala.org/work/freedom/lbr.html
The American Library Association affirms that all libraries are forums for information and ideas, and that basic policies should guide their services.
American Library Association Freedom of Information Act
www.ftrf.org/foia.html
This Web site links to Information on the First Amendment and intellectual freedom, and additional information on the Freedom of Information Act.
Code of Ethics of the American Library Association
www.ala.org/alaorg/oif/ethics.html
Ethical dilemmas occur when values are in conflict. The American Library Association Code of Ethics states the values to which libraries are committed, and embodies the ethical responsibilities of the profession in this changing information environment.
Freedom to Read Statement
www.ala.org/alaorg/oif/freeread.html
This Web site discusses the freedom to read as essential to our democracy and points out that it is continuously under attack.

Classification Systems

Let's Do Dewey
www.mtsu.edu/~vvesper/dewey.html
Middle Tennessee State University (Murfreesboro) *offers an excellent overview of the Dewey Decimal System.*
Library of Congress Classification Outline
http://lcweb.loc.gov/catdir/cpso/lcco/lcco.html
This site offers the letters and titles of the main classes of the Library of Congress Classification. One may merely click on any class to view an outline of its subclasses.

Virtual Libraries

Education Virtual Library
www.csu.edu.au/education/library.html
This Web site provides information via a virtual university from Charles Sturt University (New South Wales, Australia).

ERAU Virtual Library

www.embryriddle.edu/libraries/virtual

This Web site is from the Embry-Riddle Aeronautical University (Daytona Beach, FL); it provides 1,911 links regarding aerospace and aviation.

The WWW Virtual Library

www.vlib.org

This site includes areas to research, from "agriculture" to "society." Note: numerous extremely specialized virtual libraries exist as well as general virtual libraries.

Chapter 5

There Is So Much Information on the Internet. Where Do I Begin?

INTRODUCTION

The Internet is like a vast, uncataloged library. Whether you are using Infoseek, Lycos, Dogpile, or any of the search or metasearch engines, you are not searching the entire Web. Web sites often promise to search everything, but they can't deliver. Moreover, what they do search is not necessarily updated regularly, regardless of what's advertised. If a librarian told you, "Here are five articles on typhoons. We have 30 others, but we're not going to let you see them until you have tried another search in another library," you'd really be irritated, huh? The Internet does this routinely, and no one seems to mind. With this in mind, let's take a closer look at how to make the Internet actually work for you.

THE INTERNET

The Internet has been in existence—changing and growing—for over 30 years. It is a network of networks, linking computers to computers. The Internet is the transport system for the information stored in various forms on countless computers. It is a massive network that consists of interconnected subnetworks worldwide. (Note: The Internet itself does not contain information. Rather than saying that a document was "found on the Internet," it would be more accurate to say that it was found "through" or "while using" the Internet.) The Internet consists of an enormous amount of unorganized information. No one individual or group manages or owns it; it is a self-publishing medium. The Internet is a clearinghouse containing materials both authentic and unauthentic.

Today, the Internet is changing at staggering rates and is becoming more readily available to everyone. No one actually knows what the long-term impact of the Internet will be.

The Internet is comprised of the World Wide Web and various text-only resources, which present information in text, graphic, video, and audio formats. The World Wide Web is estimated to contain approximately four billion documents. When you "search" the Web, you are not actually searching it directly. The Web is the totality of the many Web "pages" that reside on computers all over the world. Your computer cannot locate or retrieve them all directly. What you are able to do through your computer is access one or more of the many intermediate search tools now available. You explore a search tool's database or collection of sites—a relatively small subset of the entire World Wide Web. When you access the Internet using a browser, you are viewing documents on the World Wide Web.

- A *browser* is a computer program (a software application, such as Netscape or Internet Explorer) that resides on your computer, enabling you to use the computer to view World Wide Web documents—to locate and display Web pages. Browsers allow you to click on hypertext links (with URLs to other pages) to retrieve information via the Web and offer additional features for navigating and managing the Web.
- A *URL* (Universal Resource Locator) is the most basic information about where a Web page is located on the World Wide Web. It includes information about which Web server the page is stored, in which directory it is located, its name, and the protocol used to retrieve it. The following is an example of what a URL looks like: *http://www.m-w.com/dictionary.htm*, which is the *Merriam-Webster Dictionary* online.
- The "http" is the protocol, or the special set of rules that end points in a telecommunication connection use when communicating; the *.com* or *.org* or *.gov*, etc. is the domain.
- "dictionary.htm" is the directory or file.
- The three-letter suffix on the end of the domain name is perhaps the most revealing part of a URL. Currently, there are a variety of such suffixes in use, the most common of which are
  - com (commercial)
  - org (organization)
  - net (business)
  - gov (government)

- mil (military)
- edu (education).

Various new domains are currently on the rise, though none of them have yet become as common as those above. Many countries also have their own national suffixes, appended at the end of the URLs of Web sites supported within their own national infrastructure.

Once a domain name is properly registered, no other person or company can use the same name. *HTML* stands for Hypertext Markup Language. It is a standardized language of computer code, containing the textual content, images, and links to other documents. On the World Wide Web, the HTML allows a text area, image, or other object to become a chain or link that retrieves another computer file on the Internet.

Searching the Internet successfully requires expertise. To find reliable, accurate information on the Internet and to navigate it efficiently and effectively, you must learn how it functions. It is important to remember that the Internet emphasizes quantity, not necessarily quality. It is an excellent tool for locating information, but it is typically not the best place to begin academic research. The World Wide Web is not indexed using any standard vocabulary. In Web searching, you are always guessing what words will be in the pages you want to find or speculating about the subject terms that someone may have chosen to organize a Web site covering a specific topic. This is the opposite of the organized system of an online public-access catalog in a library, which uses standard vocabulary and is much easier to search.

SEARCHING EFFICIENTLY AND EFFECTIVELY

The only easy and certain way to find the location of information on the Internet is to already know where it exists. This is difficult, however, because there is no complete index to the resources available on the Internet. Sometimes finding Web documents or sites can be fairly simple, other times it seems impossibly difficult. This is partly because of its sheer size, but it is also because it is not indexed like a library catalog. Actually, no one knows how many individual files reside on the Internet. In order to conduct research on the Internet, you must understand a variety of search tools that will assist you in finding the information desired.

There are three basic types of search tools: (1) search engines, (2) subject directories, and (3) the "Invisible (or Deep) Web. Search engines are built by computer robot programs, are not organized by subject categories, are exceptionally large, and are not evaluated. Subject directories are built by human selection, organized into subject categories, small and specialized, and often carefully evaluated and annotated. The Invisible Web consists of pages that cannot be found in search engines and are rarely in subject directories, offering two to three times as many pages as the "visible" Web. These tools can unearth the vast resources of the Internet. It is vital to pick the right starting place, that is, the right search tools, as it will result in a more targeted result. Note the following five concerns before conducting your search:

- Many people use search engines without considering the usefulness of subject directories (discussed later in this chapter) for their topics.
- The difference between the three types of tools is often poorly understood.
- The Deep, or Invisible, Web is growing at a phenomenal rate, so its content is becoming increasingly important to researchers.
- All of these tools complement each other in the research process.
- The lines are blurring between which sites offer which resources (for example, it is common to find directories and specialized searches on the Deep Web at many search engine sites).

Prior to beginning the research process, it is important to review the information discussed in Chapters 2 and 3 concerning subject and topic selection, as well as search strategies and techniques. You will find it necessary to explore multiple sites when you are investigating a topic. Search engines and subject directories vary in their contents, features, selectivity, accuracy, and retrieval technologies. In addition, the world of subject directories and search engines is a highly volatile one. Do not be dismayed if you visit a site and discover that things have changed. This is par for the course. Many of these sites are commercial enterprises and competition is keen. When changes occur, they are often for the better, as the service attempts to keep ahead of the pack. How do you actually locate information on the Internet? The following are some possible methods:

- Go directly to the site if you have the address (URL).
- Explore a subject directory.
- Conduct a search using a Web search engine.
- Explore the information stored in live databases on the Web (Deep or Invisible Web).

It is critical that you view numerous sites when researching a topic using the Internet. Do not rely on only one Web site or one type of site.

     Exercise 5.1: Searching the Internet

As we have learned, the Internet is made up of millions of search engines, subject directories, and invisible Web sites, along with online databases and so forth.

Using the following Internet sites, search for "medicare" in each and answer the questions that follow.

www.yahoo.com (Subject Directory)
www.infomine.com (Subject Directory)
www.dogpile.com (Search Engine)
www.lycos.com (Search Engine)
www.profusion.com (Invisible Web)

Did you locate different information in these Web sites? If so, what? Be specific. Why do you believe different information might exist on these Web sites?

SEARCH ENGINES

There is no way for anyone to search the entire Web, and any search tool that claims that it offers it all to you is distorting the truth. That being understood, one way to locate information on the Internet is to use a search engine. Search engines are searchable databases of Internet files collected by a computer program. The indexing is created from the collected files (e.g., title, full-text, size, etc.). There are no selection criteria for the files themselves although evaluation can be applied to the ranking. A search engine allows you to enter keywords relating to the topic and retrieve information about Internet sites containing those keywords. Remember that all search engines have rules for formulating queries. Read the "help files" at each site before proceeding.

Directories (discussed in detail later in this chapter) such as Yahoo, are designed for identifying general information. Similar to a library catalog, they classify Web sites into similar categories, such as natural history museums or accounting firms, and so on. The results of your search will be a list of Web sites related to your specific search term. For instance, if you are looking for the Louvre Web site, use a directory. However, what if you want more specific information, such as biographical information about Leonardo da Vinci? Web indexes are the way to go because they search the entire contents of a Web site. Indexes use software programs (called spiders and robots) that scour the Internet, analyzing millions of Web pages and indexing all of the words. Indexes such as Google and AltaVista find individual pages of a Web site that match your search criteria, even if the site itself has nothing to do with what you are looking for. Be prepared to wade through enormous amounts of irrelevant information when searching indexes.

Search engines do not search the Internet itself. They search databases of information about the Internet that the company hosting the search engine has developed. Each search engine looks through a different database. That is why you retrieve different sites from exactly the same terms (keywords) in different search engines. For targeted, complex, and sometimes general queries, use a search engine. There are at least two ways a search engine finds out about a document and enters it into its database. One way is for the publisher of the document to register it with the search engine. The second is for the search-engine company to find it as part of its research routines. (Note: Some pages and links are excluded from most search engines. This will be discussed later in this chapter.) Search engines provide easy-to-use forms on which you enter keywords or phrases. Subject categories help you narrow your search terms and strategies, and advanced searching capabilities increase the chances of a more relevant list. There are numerous search engines and each one differs greatly.

You can receive better results from an Internet search engine if you know when to use it. So, when should you use a search engine?

Use a search engine

- when you have a narrow or obscure topic or idea to research;
- when you are looking for a specific site;
- when you want to retrieve a large number of documents on your topic;
- when you want to search for particular types of documents, file types, source locations, languages, date last modified, etc; or
- when you want to take advantage of newer retrieval technologies, such as concept clustering, ranking by popularity, link ranking, etc.

A meta-search engine is a search tool that does not create its own database of information, but instead searches those of other search engines. Metacrawler is a good example. It searches the databases of Lycos, WebCrawler, Excite, AltaVista, and Yahoo! Meta-search engines quickly and superficially search several individual search engines at once and returns results compiled into a sometimes-convenient format. However, they only catch about 10 percent of the search results in any of the search engines they visit.

Every person searches for information differently and has favorite resources, whether they are print, nonprint, or Web sites. Good searching begins well before you enter the topic terms into a search engine. Critical thinking capabilities are as necessary in using a search engine as they are in using any print resource or database. Searching the Internet requires knowledge.

In order to determine which search engines you prefer, view Figure 5.1.

Search Engine	**Google** www.google.com	**Yahoo! Search** search.yahoo.com	**Teoma** www.teoma.com
Links to help	Google help pages	Yahoo! help pages	Teoma help pages
Size, type Size varies frequently and widely. See tests and more charts.	HUGE. Size not disclosed in any way that allows comparison. Probably the biggest. Biggest in tests.	HUGE. Claims over 20 billion total "web objects."	LARGE. Claims to have 2 billion fully indexed, searchable pages. Strives to become #1 in size.
Noteworthy features and limitations	Popularity ranking using PageRank™. Indexes the first 101KB of a Web page, and 120KB of PDF's. ~ before a word finds synonyms sometimes (~help > FAQ, tutorial, etc.)	Shortcuts give quick access to dictionary, synonyms, patents, traffic, stocks, encyclopedia, and more.	Subject-Specific Popularity™ ranking. Suggests terms within results to refine Suggests pages within results with many links.
Phrase searching (term definition)	Yes. Use " ". Searches common "stop words" if in phrases in quotes.	Yes. Use " "	Yes. Use " ". Searches common "stop words" if in phrases in quotes.
Boolean logic (term definition)	Partial. AND assumed between words. Capitalize OR. —excludes. No ( ) or nesting. In Advanced Search, partial Boolean available in boxes.	Accepts AND, OR, NOT or AND NOT, and ( ). Must be capitalized. You **must** enclose terms joined by OR in parentheses (classic Boolean).	Partial. AND assumed between words. Capitalize OR. —excludes. No ( ) or nesting.
+Requires/ -Excludes (term definition)	—excludes + will allow you to retrieve "stop words" (e.g., +in)	—excludes + will allow you to search common words: "+in truth"	—excludes + will allow you to retrieve "stop words" (e.g., +in)
Sub-searching (term definition)	Sort of. At bottom of results page, click "Search within results" and enter more terms. Adds terms.	Add terms.	Sort of. Add terms. REFINE pastes suggested sub-topics within results.

Figure 5.1   Search Engines: Table of Features

(continued on next page)

Results ranking (term definition)	Based on page popularity measured in links to it from other pages: high rank if a lot of other pages link to it. Fuzzy AND also invoked. Matching and ranking based on "cached" version of pages that may not be the most recent version.	Automatic Fuzzy AND.	Based on Subject-Specific Popularity™, links to a page by related pages. More info.
Field limiting (term definition)	link: site: intitle: inurl: Advanced Search boxes for most of these. Offers Uncle Sam for US federal pages and other special searches.	link: site: intitle: inurl: url: hostname: (Explanation of these distinctions.)	intitle: inurl: site: geoloc: Explanations, limitations.
Truncation, Stemming (term definition)	No truncation. Stems some words. Search variant endings and synonyms separately, separating with OR (capitalized): airline OR airlines	Neither. Search with OR as in Google.	Neither. Search with OR as in Google.
Case sensitivity (term definition)	No.	No.	No.
Language	Yes. Major Romanized and non-Romanized languages in Advanced Search.	Yes. Major Romanized and non-Romanized languages.	Yes. Major Romanized languages. Use lang:
Limit by age of documents	In Advanced Search.	In Advanced Search.	In Advanced Search.
Translation	Yes, in Translate this page link following some pages. To and sometimes from English and major European languages and Chinese, Japanese, Korean.	Yes.	No.

Figure 5.1   Search Engines: Table of Features (Taken from http://www.lib. berkeley.edu/TeachingLib/Guides/Internet/SearchEngines.html, reproduced with permission.)

Search engines offer different information, different types of searching, different subject material . . . they broaden your horizons just a little more—dig in!

SUBJECT DIRECTORIES

Subject directories are subject "trees" that catalog or create classification schema for selected Web sites, organizing Internet sites by subject. Researchers who are starting with broad topics use directories to move from general information to more specific subsets of the information by accessing subfolders within the classification schema. Unlike search engines, which perform keyword searches that are created by specific software programs, subject directories are built by humans (hand selected and evaluated carefully); not computer programs. If you want to view Web sites that experts in a particular field recommend, use a subject directory. This allows you to choose a subject of interest and then browse the list of resources in that category. You conduct your search by selecting a series of progressively narrower search terms from a number of lists of descriptors provided in the directory. It is important to understand that a subject directory will not have links to every piece of information on the Internet, and they are much smaller than search-engine databases. Each subject directory has unique content and a unique emphasis. They are most useful when you are trying to narrow your topic, have a broad idea to research, or want to see a list of sites recommended by experts. Two general subject directories are Yahoo! and Librarians' Internet Index.

- *Yahoo!:* This commercial portal is the largest and most famous around. It provides limited descriptions and annotations, uses phrase searching (" ") and allows subject searching.
- *Librarians' Index to the Internet:* This directory includes over 17,000 entries. It is compiled by library experts and uses highest quality sites only. It offers good and reliable annotations and allows Boolean searching.

There are some important points to keep in mind when using subject directories.

- There are two basic kinds of directories: academic/professional and commercial. Academic and professional directories are created and maintained by subject experts to support the needs of researchers. Commercial portals cater to the general public and are competing for traffic. Be sure you use the directory that appropriately meets your needs.
- Subject directories differ significantly in selectivity. Consider the policies of any directory that you visit.
- Many people do not make enough use of subject directories. Instead, they go straight to search engines. Keep in mind that academic subject directories contain carefully chosen and annotated lists of quality Internet sites.

When should you use a subject directory? Use a subject directory

- when you have a broad topic or idea to research;
- when you want to see a list of Web sites on your topic that experts have recommended and annotated;
- when you want to retrieve a list of sites relevant to your topic rather than numerous individual pages contained within these sites;
- when you want to search for the site title, annotation, and (if available) assigned keywords to retrieve relevant material rather than the full-text document; or
- when you want to avoid viewing low-content documents that often turn up on search engines.

Asking whether search engines or subject directories are better cannot yield an objective answer. It depends on your personal preferences and immediate needs. Some people like subject directories because they can control the search pattern. Directories also allow you to browse and to be more general with your search terms. Search engines leave the searching pattern to the computer program and can be used to locate resources that are more specific. One weakness of subject directories is that you must depend on the descriptors provided by the company. A weakness of search engines is the unnecessarily extensive number of "hits" they can produce.

Exercise 5.2: Subject Directories

In order to understand subject directories more thoroughly, let's visit a few. This will allow you to decide if you prefer subject directories or search engines—or *both*, for their specific assistance. While you are visiting these sites, think of the following:

1. Do the annotations provide sufficient information?
2. Does it contain any full-text resources?
3. What type of searching does it use (phrase, Boolean, etc.)?
4. Is it user-friendly?

Yahoo! *www.yahoo.com*

Yahoo! is the original search directory. You can go from broader topics to narrower ones.

Librarians' Internet Index *www.lii.org*

This is a subject directory compiled by public librarians in the information-supply business. It is of high quality and has reliable, useful annotations.

Do you see the difference between search engines and subject directories? Write down how you would describe the difference to a friend.

_____

_____

_____

Now, list three ways you could use a subject directory while working on a research paper:

1. _____

2. _____

3. _____

Ok, here are some more subject directories to explore:

Infomine   *http://infomine.ucr.edu*

Academic Info   *www.academicinfo.net*

List one thing you liked about each:

Infomine: _____

Academic Info: _____

THE INVISIBLE WEB

The concept of the "Invisible," or "Deep," Web has emerged with the rise of the public Web. This refers to content that is stored in databases accessible on the Web but not available via search engines. In other words, this content is invisible to search engines because spiders or robots cannot or will not enter into databases and extract content from them as they can from static Web pages. The only way to access information on the Deep Web is to search the databases themselves. Topical coverage runs the gamut from scholarly resources to commercial entities. Very current, dynamically changing information is likely to be stored in these databases, including news, job listings, airline flights, etc. As the number of Web-accessible databases grow, it will be essential to use them to conduct successful research on the Web. When dealing with the Invisible Web, keep the following in mind:

- Many databases on the Web are searchable from their own sites. A good directory will link to these sites.
- There are Web sites that specialize in collecting links to databases available on the Web.
- Topical coverage on the Invisible Web is extremely varied. This presents a challenge, since it is impossible to anticipate what might turn up in a database. In addition, because databases proliferate on the Web, the coverage will be fluid.
- Information that is dynamically changing in content will appear on the Deep Web. Examples are news, job postings, and similar topical information.
- Directories are a part of the Invisible Web. A few examples are phone books and other "people finders"; lists of professionals, such as doctors and lawyers; patents; and dictionary definitions.

Information indexed on the Invisible Web includes, but is not limited to

- e-mail addresses
- dictionaries and other reference books
- BBC news archive
- FAA Flight Tracker
- product catalogs
- contents of library catalogs
- streaming media

- Java Script
- contents of Web-based databases such as *ERIC*

The Invisible Web contains some of the most authoritative information on the Internet. This information is usually free. The problem is that search engines can't find it.

When should you use the Invisible Web? Use the Invisible Web:

- when you want dynamically changing content, or
- when you want to find information that is normally stored in a database, such as a phone book listing, geographical data, etc.

(The above information can be printed from the companion Web site.)

Do you understand the concept of the Invisible Web now? Ok, let's review. There are basically three ways to access information on the Internet (basically!): search engines, like AskJeeves; subject directories, like Yahoo!; and the Invisible Web, like the Web site ProFusion. The Invisible Web contains information that you cannot find on either a search engine or a subject directory. Sounds mysterious, but if you look at the site ProFusion (www.profusion.com), it will become clearer. Also, view the following chart to clarify questions you may have regarding Visible and Invisible Web sites.

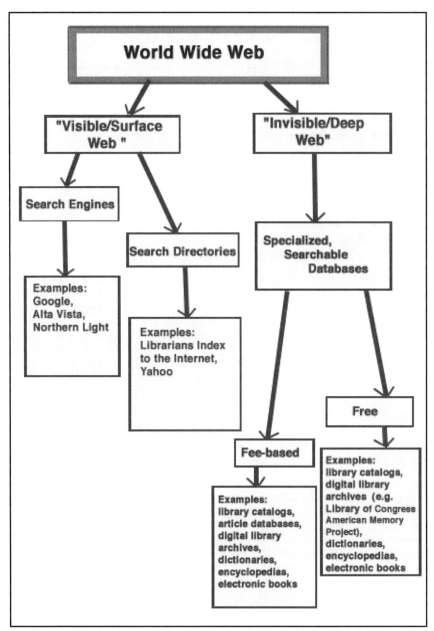

Figure 5.2 Visible Web versus Invisible Web (Taken from www.kn.pacbell.com/ wired/21stcent/wversus.html, reproduced with permission.)

Exercise 5.3: The Invisible Web

There are many, many invisible Web sites. One is "IncyWincy" at www.incywincy.com.
Go to the IncyWincy Web site.
Type in the name of your favorite actor or actress.
Explore the information provided and all links.

1. What information did you find on this site that you could not find on Google?
2. What information did you find on this site that you could not find on Alta Vista?
3. Do you like this Web site? Why or why not?

The Internet is a worldwide computer network that has forever changed the way people receive and transmit information. Its global nature facilitates communication among people of all nationalities in every country on the planet. Everyone is a potential message receiver and provider in this two-way communication system. As wonderful as the Internet is in providing an unbelievable wealth of information, it can also be an electronic nightmare for those who do not know how to use it properly. Three ways to more efficiently sift through the masses of information are (1) search engines, (2) subject directories, and (3) the Invisible Web. These tools assist in alleviating the potential thousands and thousands of hits one might receive using any one search term or phrase. Further, they make Internet searching easier, more efficient, and more effective for your specific research.

REFERENCES AND FURTHER READING

Bates, Mary Ellen. 2004. "Tapping into the Brains of the Web." *EContent*, 27: 6.
Bruce, Christine. 1997. *Seven Faces of Information Literacy*. Queensland, South Australia: AUSLIB Press.
Clyde, A. 2002. "The Invisible Web." *Teacher Librarian*, 29: 4.
Cusumano, Michael A. 2005. "Google: What It Is and What It Is Not." *Communications of the ACH*, 48: 2.
Descy, Don E. 2004. "Searching the Web: From the Visible to the Invisible." *Tech Trends*, 48: 1.
Gogolski, Adam. 2004. "Uncloaking the Invisible Web." *Louisville*, 11: 8.

Grimes, B. 2002. "Expand Your Web Search Horizons." *PC World,* 20: 6.
Gunn, Holly. 2004. "With Specialty Search Engines." *Teacher Librarian,* 32: 2.
Hane, Paula J. 2005. "The Latest on Blogs, Search Engines, and Content Integration." *Information Today,* 22: 1.
Jasco, Peter. 2002. "Northern Light Still Shine On." *Information Today,* 19: 30.
Levy, Steven. 2002, 25 March. "Faster Than the Rest." *Newsweek,* 139: 48.
McLaughlin, L., and T. Spring. 2004. "The Straight Story on Search Engines." *PC World,* 20: 7.
Mitchoff, Kate Houston. 2002. "Explorers." *Library Journal,* 127: 37.
Notess, Greg R. 2002. "Internet Search Engine Update." *Online,* 26: 20.
Rosato, Donna. 2004. "Start Your Search Engines." *Money,* 33:12.
Schrock, Kathy. 2003. "The Search Continues." *School Library Journal* (March) 49: 2.
Sherman, Chris, and Gary Price. 2001. *The Invisible Web: Uncovering Information Sources Search Engines Can't See.* Medford, NJ: CyberAge Books.
Strand, Jill. 2004. "Web Sites Worth a Click." *Information Outlook,* 8: 10.
Young, Jeffrey R. 2004. "Google Unveils a Search Engine Focused on Scholarly Materials." *Chronicle of Higher Education,* 51: 15.

WEBLIOGRAPHY

The Internet

Internet Public Library
www.ipl.org
IPL provides library services and resources such as reference and links to free online books and articles.
Internet Scout Project
http://scout.wisc.edu
This Web site provides timely information to the education community about valuable Internet resources.
Internet Search Tools—Quick Reference Guide
www.itrc.ucf.edu/conferences/pres/srchtool.html
This useful Web site explains when to use which search engine, subject directory, and so forth.

Invisible Web

IncyWincy
www.incywincy.com
This invisible Web site offers 50 million pages that are spidered and indexed, as well as hundreds of thousands of search engines that are indexed and searchable.
The Invisible Web Directory
www.invisible-web.net
This Web site is a companion to "The Invisible Web: Finding Hidden Internet Resources Search Engines Can't See" by Chris Sherman and Gary Price.

Invisible Web: What It Is, Why It Exists, How to Find It, and Its Inherent Ambiguity
www.lib.berkeley.edu/TeachingLib/Guides/Internet/InvisibleWeb.html
The Invisible Web is what you cannot retrieve ("see") in the search results and other links contained in subject directories and search engines.
Those Dark Hiding Places: The Invisible Web Revealed
http://library.rider.edu/scholarly/rlackie/Invisible/Inv_Web.html
This article notes that "Although many popular search engines boast about their ability to index information on the Web, more of it has become invisible to their searching spiders."

Subject Directories

Finding Information on the Web: Subject Directories
www.wesleyan.edu/libr/tut/websearch/directories.html
This Web site explains, "Subject directories are collections of Internet resources organized into subject categories, usually arranged from general to more specific subjects. They are an efficient means to locate Web resources by topic. Subject directories are useful if you are looking for a broad or general topic, or if you are unfamiliar with a topic and you want sites recommended by subject specialists. Many directories also provide evaluations of the sites they index, and/or allow you to perform a keyword search to find indexed sites."
Academic Info
www.academicinfo.net
This Web site provides students, educators, and librarians with an online subject directory to access quality, relevant, and current Internet resources on each academic discipline.
Infomine
http://infomine.ucr.edu
This subject directory is a virtual library of Internet resources relevant to faculty, students, and research staff at the university level.
Internet Subject Directories
http://library.albany.edu/internet/subject.html
This Web site offers academic and professional directories as well as commercial directories and portals.
Librarians' Internet Index
http://lii.org
This is a subject directory that provides reliable librarian-selected resources.
Recommended Subject Directories
www.lib.berkeley.edu/TeachingLib/Guides/Internet/SubjDirectories.html
This useful chart compares the subject directories Infomine, Librarians' Index, Academic Info, About.com, Google and Yahoo!.
Using Subject Directories: A Tutorial
www.learnwebskills.com/search/subject.html

This Web site states, "Because directories cover only a small fraction of the pages available on the Web, they are most effective for finding general information on popular or scholarly subjects. If you are looking for something specific, use a search engine."

WebData

www.webdata.com

This site offers a collection of searchable databases on the Web, organized into topics maintained by ExperTelligence, Inc.

Search Engines

Direct Search

www.freepint.com/gary/direct.htm

"Direct Search is a growing compilation of links to the search interfaces of resources that contain data not easily or entirely searchable/accessible from general search tools like Alta Vista, Google, or Hotbot."

How Search Engines Work

searchenginewatch.com/webmasters/article.php/2168031

This site was created by Danny Sullivan and includes basic information regarding search engines and how they work.

Search Engine Watch

www.searchenginewatch.com

Search Engine Watch provides a wealth of useful information, such as "Web Searching Tips," "Search Engine Listings," "Search Engine Resources," and so forth.

Which Search Engine?

http://library.queensu.ca/inforef/instruct/search.htm

This Web site discusses search engines and subject directories.

Chapter 6

How Do I Know If
What I Read Is True?

With the tools, tips, and ideas from the previous chapters at hand, it should be easy for you to track down information about virtually everything you want to know. The trouble is that there is always the possibility that the information you've found is inaccurate, out-of-date, prejudiced, or otherwise unreliable. This chapter covers the evaluation of resources, discussing a variety of strategies to help you determine if what you have is really what you want.

WHY EVALUATION IS IMPORTANT

As the various forms of producing and distributing information multiply, the origins of the information they convey tends to become increasingly obscure. While many publishers and publications still go through processes of approval and verification for everything they release, this is not necessarily the case with information found on the Internet or through other sources, such as video, CD-ROM, and DVD. Even scholarly publications can contain inaccuracies if they are not up-to-date. Keep in mind that when people use the old maxim, "I read it in the paper; it must be true!" they are usually joking. Making use of anything you have read or seen without thinking about its accuracy is always a bad idea.

The massive amount of material available on the Internet can make it tempting to use what you find there without looking further, but you always do so at your own risk. Consider, for example, the popular Web site Wikipedia, an encyclopedia written and edited by its readers. While much of the information it contains is accurate, it is also subject to malicious misuse, meaning that to use facts from it without verification is a dicey proposition at best.

Fortunately, evaluation is something that you already do almost on a daily basis without even realizing it. For example, when you watch a television program, don't you think about how much you like or dislike it? Likewise, when visiting a new restaurant, you will probably think about the way it measures up to others you have visited. While these comparative exercises may not seem especially complex, this kind of thinking is the fundamental basis of evaluation. Sometimes you evaluate things in your daily lives in a more formal way. For instance, you probably research a variety of cars before purchasing one. This same evaluation procedure is also important when conducting academic research; it helps you develop a high-quality product. For this reason, evaluation of print, nonprint, and Internet information is an extremely important aspect of research—and of *learning to learn*.

FOUR KEY CRITERIA FOR EVALUATING INFORMATION

Specific criteria can assist you with the evaluation of resources—and make it easier for you to choose the "best" ones for your specific needs. There are four criteria you can use to evaluate information. Each one helps you to examine a different aspect of the work. These criteria are accuracy and authority, objectivity, currency, and scope.

Accuracy and Authority

The first step is to determine the accuracy and authority of your source. Indicators of authority include the education and experience of the authors, editors, and contributors, as well as the reputation of the publisher or sponsoring agency. Evaluating print resources is considerably easier than evaluating nonprint and Web-based materials. Why? Because in print publications, much of the information needed for evaluation is provided in an easy-to-locate and easy-to-read manner. Let's consider a reference book (for example, a handbook). Who are the authors, editors, contributors, and publishers of the source? What credentials do they have and what kind of reputations? What else have they created? The answers to these questions are usually straightforward because statements of authorship can usually be found on the title page and verso (back) of the title page. Occasionally, front matter (title page; verso or the reverse, or left-hand, page of a book; preface; and introduction) or an "About-the-Author" section will provide information on the author's credentials, affiliations, other works, honors. In other words, you can assume that a printed resource from an established publisher, such as Macmillan, is reliable; others have conducted the evaluation for you.

On the other hand, it can be extremely difficult to discover who actually provided the information on an electronic Web site. Locating author information for Web pages frequently involves "going back a layer or two" in the Web site (for example, using links to locate information about the author or creator). Some items to look for include who provided the information, why, and explicit statements of authority.

Objectivity

The objectivity and fairness of a source are also important considerations in the evaluation of resources. Objectivity includes coverage of the topics provided (the goals and objectives have to be clearly stated to determine coverage) and the factual, objective, and unbiased nature of the information. Ask yourself if the author or contributor have biases. How reliable are the facts presented? This can be a bit tougher than establishing authority—even for print resources. However, print materials often have a statement of purpose that fundamentally helps to answer these questions. You can usually find this in the preface, introduction, or table of contents. Nonetheless, in many print resources establishing the level of objectivity and bias is more complicated than that.

One effective way to discover if a work is biased is to look at the coverage of controversial issues and the balance of coverage given to various subjects. For example, if you are researching the subject of abortion, ask if the author is pro-choice, pro-life, or unbiased. You might read the material briefly to check about the author (his or her credentials, etc.). See what the chapter titles are like. Remember, however, that biased material can also be a valuable part of your research as long as you acknowledge the fact of the bias and do not treat it as absolutely and unproblematically true.

Here are some other tips for ascertaining bias in print materials:

1. Check the illustrations for balance of presentation.
2. Check the content for disparaging comments or slanted perspectives.
3. Watch for loaded words, such as "primitive," "savage," "lazy," "evil," "ignorant," etc.
4. Look at the copyright date and consider how attitudes may have changed since the resource was created.

For online sources, consider if a Web site was developed as a means of advertising or to present scholarly material? The creator of the information may serve as an indicator of biases on electronic sites. For example, was it created by a corporation? If so, for example, by Disney, it could be biased towards Disney products and services.

Currency

All resources should be checked for currency, which is fairly straightforward with print resources. The copyright date is normally (and should be) on the title page or verso. Consider whether there is a more current edition, or is this the most up-to-date information concerning the topic you are researching. Also check the bibliography and footnotes. Were they current at the time of publication? Although identifying currency in print materials is rarely difficult, you must also look at other resources (print, nonprint, and Internet) to locate the most up-to-date information for your particular research project. For example, if you are writing a research paper regarding the effects of the Internet on personal communication using statistics from 1994, your information will clearly be out-of-date.

In establishing the currency of relevant information on an electronic site, check document headers and footers. Look for posting and revision dates, policy statements on information maintenance, and link maintenance. It is also significant to recognize that there is no guarantee that a particular page will reside in the same location today as it did yesterday. If you plan to use the information and cite it, a good strategy is to note the date and time you visit the site.

Scope

Scope refers to the basic breadth-and-depth question: What is covered and in what detail? The scope should reflect the purpose of the resource and its intended audience. Has the creator of the information accomplished what was intended? Aspects of scope include subject, geographic location, and time period. Evaluating scope includes reviewing topical aspects of the subject of the resource and noting if there are any key omissions. For example, let's assume you are conducting research on wars from 1950—2000. One resource you consult does not include the Gulf War. What does this say about the scope of this material? However, one should keep in mind that a lack of scope does not mean the material is lacking in depth. Discovering the scope of a resource may take a little time, but it is well worth the effort.

For printed materials, the statement of purpose is generally found in the preface or introduction, and you can use this as a reference point when evaluating scope. For an electronic resource, look for the stated purpose on the site, along with any limitations that may apply and any comments on the site's comprehensiveness. Information about nonprint resources, such as CD-ROMs and DVDs, can often be found in the publisher's or vendor's descriptive materials.

Evaluation of resources is vital in today's world. Prior to the evolution of the computer, most materials were evaluated for you before you viewed them. This is no longer true. The goal of using these evaluative criteria is to establish if the material you located (on the Internet, in particular) is accurate and useful for your research.

Now that you have learned about the fundamentals of evaluating resources, let's find out if this sounds more difficult than it is. You will probably find that it is not necessarily a particularly time-consuming or complex task. Try to evaluate a print resource on your own by doing Exercise 6.1 "Evaluating a Print Resource."

Exercise 6.1: Evaluating a Print Resource

Locate any reference book. (Ask a librarian for assistance, if necessary.) Look at the information in the front of the book (title and verso pages, preface, and introduction) and answer the questions for each section. Following the questions are tips (in italics) to help you answer each question:

1. **Look at the title and verso pages.** *(The title page is usually the first page in a book. It gives information about the creators, publishers, and copyright.)*
   Question: Who is the author or creator of this print material?
   Tip: *This information should be included either on the title or verso page. The verso page may also include useful information such as the International Standard Book Number (ISBN), the Library of Congress Cataloging-in-Publication (CIP) Data, the record number, and miscellaneous information, such if it includes a companion Web site or CD-ROM.*
   Question: What else has the author or creator written on this subject or related topics?
   Tip: *Again, this information may be in the front portion of the book. You should also check biographical sources, such as* Biography and Genealogy Master Index, *or you can visit* www.google.com *and enter the author's name. Remember, you can always ask a librarian for assistance. Be careful if you use Google for author information. Many people have the same name—there may even be two authors with the same name! Conduct your research wisely.*
   Question: What edition is this resource?
   Tip: *If the book is not the first edition, look on the cover of the book, the title page, or on the verso page—for something like 2nd ed. or revised edition.*
   Question: Who published this resource?
   Tip: *The publisher information should be located on the verso of the title page.*
   Question: Is the publisher reputable?
   Tip: *This information may be difficult to locate. Generally, you know if a publisher is reputable because you have heard of them—for example, National Geographic. If you do not recognize the name, you might call a librarian or search the Internet for further information about this publisher. You may also locate the publisher's Web site. Again, use your evaluative criteria when viewing this site.*

(continued on next page)

Exercise 6.1: Evaluating a Print Resource (*Continued*)

2. Now read the preface or introduction of the material.
Question: What is the purpose for writing this resource?
Tip: *The purpose should be stated at the beginning in the preface or introduction. This is very important. Typically, good resources include exceptional introductions, prefaces, or both. The purpose should be clear and concise.*
Question: Are the goals and objectives clearly stated?
Tip: *The goals and objectives will normally appear in the preface. They should be clear and concise, for example, "This book explains 'Feng Shui,' the Chinese way to harmony." More precise objectives should follow the goal statement. Again, this is vitally important.*
Question: Does this source use correct grammar, spelling, and sentence structure?
Tip: *For this, you will need to scan the material. Begin this process by looking at the preface or introduction, taking note of any problematic spelling, grammar, and sentence structure as you do so. These are indicators of scholarly—or nonscholarly—materials. It may not seem that important to you, but any resource that is worth using must meet these criteria. Would you believe a material is scholarly if it is full of misspelled words?*
Question: Who is the audience?
Tip: *Check the preface or introduction. You should find why the material was written, what follows in the text, specialized language or jargon, and other pertinent information. For example, "This textbook is for undergraduate and graduate students studying to be school library media specialists." Again, this should be crystal clear and concise.*
Question: Does the author or creator have a bias(es)? If so, what? How do you know?
Tip: *Answering this can be a bit difficult. First, note the author and publisher. If the publisher is the Pro-Choice Association, this would be a clue. Next, check the preface or introduction, which explains what the resource is all about. If you still can't find this information, scan the resource to see if it includes controversial issues, dated illustrations, slanted perspectives, and loaded words (such as "primitive" or "savage"). Also note the copyright date. There may be times when you want to see "all sides" of an issue; this is fine. Therefore, bias is not necessarily a bad thing, but, nonetheless, be cautious.*
Question: Does the resource provide balanced representations of cultural, ethnic, and racial groups? How can you tell?

(continued on next page)

Exercise 6.1: Evaluating a Print Resource (Continued)
Tip: *Again, this may not be immediately apparent. It is part of determining bias, so take another look at author, publisher, preface, table of contents, and illustrations. Any or all of these may assist you in assessing balance.*   **Question:** How did the author or creator obtain the data? Is this possible to determine?   **Tip:** *If this information is available, it should be included in the preface or introduction. Otherwise, attempt to contact the creator to determine how the data was obtained. This is not always a critical issue; it depends on the research topic. This is especially important if the author claims to have made new discoveries that have yet to be covered elsewhere.*   **Question:** Are the contents based on personal opinion, research, interviews, or case studies?   **Tip:** *Again, if this information is available, it should be in the preface or introduction. For instance, it might state, "The information in this book is based on the culmination of research studies conducted by X and Y.*   **3. Look at the table of contents.**   **Question:** Are there significant attachments or appendixes? If so, what are they? Are they useful or necessary?   **Tip:** *The table of contents can tell you a great deal about the resource. First, it should be easy to follow. There should be a sufficient number of subheadings to provide a broad outline. Look at the appendixes or attachments. Do they relate to the content or are they merely "add-ons." Do they provide additional, useful information?*   **Question:** Does the resource contain a table of contents, preface, introduction, glossary, or index?   **Tip:** *This is easy; merely scan the book. A table of contents is a must to guide you through the material. The preface or introduction is particularly useful in that it explains why the resource was written and what it is about. Glossaries are helpful for sources with unfamiliar or technical terms. An index can assist you in locating particular information quickly.*   **4. Read through some of the book.**   **Question:** Is the information clear, comprehensive, and easy to read?   **Tip:** *Scan the resource. It should be easy to follow, with appropriate headings and subheadings. The words should not be too technical for you, and it should be long enough and broad enough to cover the subject or topic. This may be difficult for you at first, but it will get easier the more you do it. You might also look for "boxed items," words in bold or italics, headings and subheadings, appendices, and so forth to get an overall idea of the resource.*

(continued on next page)

Exercise 6.1: Evaluating a Print Resource (*Continued*)

Question: If visuals are used, are they useful and unambiguous?

Tip: *Illustrations can be very helpful—or they can be purely aesthetic. Visuals should complement the text, explaining it more thoroughly or more clearly.*

5. **How does it compare with other materials?**

Question: Is the information still accurate? How do you know? (Have you viewed other materials?)

Tip: *This requires more work, including looking at additional resources. Many things—for example, technology, geography, medicine—change so rapidly that in addition to checking the copyright date, you should compare it with other sources. Often Internet sources are helpful, as they tend to be current—but be certain that they are accurate, as well. Avoid locating one item and "calling it quits." If you have little knowledge about the topic, you may find that the item you selected is inaccurate and useless for your research. Remember, research takes work!*

Question: Was the print resource reviewed? Where does the review appear? Is it positive or negative?

Tip: *This may take a little looking. Ask your librarian for assistance with locating review sources. Reviews may be found online, for example, on amazon.com. Remember, however, that review sources vary from informal to scholarly—for example, a review in* New York Times Book Review *would probably be more valid than one by a reader on amazon.com.*

Hopefully, you know more now than you did before about evaluating print resources. Keep working—practice makes perfect!

EVALUATING NONPRINT INFORMATION

Hope Tillman (2001), Director of Libraries at Babson College (Babson Park, MA), explains that the growth of information on the Internet and the development of more sophisticated searching tools have made it more likely that one can find information and answers to real questions. However, within the chaos of networked data are not only valuable pieces of information but also an incredible amount of rubbish.

When evaluating nonprint materials, such as videotapes, CD-ROMs, and DVDs, the same four evaluation criteria apply. It is worth the effort because these formats are available in libraries and for purchase and present useful information in a different way. You will need to alter the criteria slightly to fit the specific format. Let's look at an example.

Exercise 6.2: Evaluating a Nonprint Resource

Select a nonprint resource, such as a CD-ROM, videocassette, audiotape, etc.

First, look at the criteria (accuracy/authority, objectivity, currency, and scope), and read the following questions while thinking about how nonprint formats differ from print formats. Following the questions are tips for answering these questions.

1. **Look at the cover and accompanying ancillary materials.**

    Question: Is the creator an expert on this subject? How do you know?

    Tip: *Just as for a print resource, reliable creators in these media are usually known. If you do not know the creator, ask other people (particularly your librarian) or attempt to locate information about the person on the Internet—for instance, via google.com.*

    Question: Who published the nonprint resource? Is it a reputable publisher? What else has this publisher produced?

    Tip: *The same approach applies for the publisher's reputation as for the creators. Do some digging around to see what you can find out.*

    Question: Are specific instructions included? Are they easy to understand?

    Tip: *Many nonprint resources include useful—or even necessary—instructions for using the materials. Like all instructions, they should be in an easy-to-understand and easy-to-use format—always look over the instructions first.*

    Question: Is technical support readily available?

    Tip: *Not all nonprint resources will require technical support, but if the format does involve technical support, it should be easily accessible at any time of the day or night. Of course, live and 24/7 is preferable.*

    Question: Are ancillary materials (such as worksheets and activity pages) included? Do you find them helpful?

    Tip: *Many nonprint materials include worksheets and activities that make the format much more useful. These materials should be complementary to the information, not simply decorative.*

    Question: Can you locate reviews of this resource? Are they positive or negative?

    Tip: *Again, reviews of nonprint materials can be found in a variety of review sources and online. Ask your librarian for a list of these sources.*

2. **View the resource.**

    Question: Is the material free of content errors?

    Tip: *Just as with print materials, nonprint resources should present correct and authoritative information. Scan the resource prior to viewing it in-depth.*

(continued on next page)

Exercise 6.2: Evaluating a Nonprint Resource (*Continued*)

Question: Does it include current information? Is there another source that is more current?

Tip: *Again, as with print sources, the information should be current. However, the copyright date is not always a good indication. View the resource, checking for up-to-date information. Enjoying the format is not enough; you need to use it for correct, objective, and current information.*

Question: Is the resource appropriate for your intended purpose?

Tip: *Although a nonprint resource may be titled "Recycling," it may only touch on one or two aspects of recycling and not be sufficient for your needs. Scan it before borrowing or purchasing it.*

Question: Is the information of sufficient scope to adequately cover your topic?

Tip: *As with print materials, the information should have enough "breadth and depth" to cover the topic you are researching.*

Question: Are the concepts and vocabulary relevant?

Tip: *At times it may be difficult to know if nonprint material is appropriate for you. The "Recycling" resource, for example, may be appropriate for elementary-school children only.*

Question: Is the resource "user friendly?"

Tip: *All nonprint materials should be easy to use and have instructions that are easy to follow. For example, be certain that it is easy to move from place to place when using a videodisc.*

Question: Is the resource objective, and does it include a balanced presentation of the topic?

Tip: *By viewing the source, you should be able to determine objectivity and bias. Listen to what is said as well as viewing the images—both can be clues.*

Question: Does the resource provide a balanced representation of cultural, ethnic, and racial groups?

Tip: *As with objectivity and bias, you can identify a balanced representation by viewing and listening to the videodisc and reading accompanying ancillary information.*

Question: Does it include appropriate, high-quality visuals? Is the sound clear?

Tip: *Just as with a print resource, the visuals should be understandable and contain information pertinent to the topic. Likewise, the sound must be clear and understandable*

As you can see, evaluating nonprint materials includes many of the same criteria and questions as evaluating print materials. However, the nature of the format requires the application of additional criteria.

To conduct accurate research, it is necessary to examine a wide variety of sources and formats and compare them with each other. Suppose you want to research global warming. It is a good idea to evaluate the information on a Web site with the information in printed periodicals and published books. A Web site on global warming may include videos, photographs, audio, a tutorial—all of which are useful in understanding this concept. Likewise, the periodical may have been written by a scholar in the field and include exceptionally current information on one or more aspects of global warming. A book on the topic might be quite comprehensive and include a history of the subject; however, it may not address the most recent information on the topic.

INTERNET EVALUATION

There are a few fundamental considerations involved with Internet research. Unlike printed sources and even other multimedia sources that must be screened, anyone with the right software and access to the Internet can publish a document on the Web, regardless of accuracy or quality of presentation. Another matter for concern is that the creator, at any time and as often as desired, can alter Web pages. What is here today may be gone tomorrow.

Remember, no matter what resource you are using, ask yourself why you are using it. Is it because it is handy? Easy to read? On the Web? Short? You should search for resources that are appropriate for the information you are seeking. Try evaluating Internet information by completing Exercise 6.3 "Evaluating Online Resources."

Exercise 6.3: Evaluating Online Resources

Let's look at the evaluation criteria (accuracy/authority, objectivity, currency, and scope)—this time with regard to the Internet. While viewing the Web site "Beef Nutrition," answer the following questions. For each question there is a tip to help you.

1. Explore the Web site *http://beefnutrition.org* **and answer the following questions (refer to the tips in italics).**

Question: Who is the author or creator of the site? Can you contact this person(s)?

Tip: *On any Web site, at the very least, the creator's name should appear along with an e-mail address. Typically, this information is found at the bottom portion of the homepage.*

Question: Is the author or creator of the Web site qualified to write this work? How do you know? Does the author have any other publications?

Tip: *Of course, this varies with the type of Web site—informational, personal, etc. However, "Beef Nutrition" should state not only who created it, but also the creator's credentials. Research the author/creator. Go to the Web site www.google.com to see if the person has created other sites or is affiliated with a reputable organization. Remember to put quotation marks around the person's name.*

Question: What are the purpose, goals, and objectives of this Web site?

Tip: *It should be easy to locate the purpose, goals, and objectives of a Web site. "Beef Nutrition" should explain why it is written, for whom it is written, and what you will learn by visiting the Web site. Look at the entire site, including all links.*

Question: Why was this site produced?

Tip: *This should be obvious from the site itself. First, check the domain (.com, .org, etc.), which may give some clues. For example, a .gov (government) site is produced for people interested in various aspects of the United States government or interested in information published by the government. Next, examine the Web site to determine its purpose. Is it for information, advertising, or aesthetics?*

Question: Who published the site? Are the publisher's qualifications on the site?

Tip: *Publisher information, like creator information, should be available on the homepage, typically at the bottom of the homepage. It does make a difference. If "Beef Nutrition" were published by the Poultry Association of America, it would be important to know that.*

(continued on next page)

Exercise 6.3: Evaluating Online Resources (*Continued*)

Question: How detailed is the information?

Tip: *Look at the entire Web site, including all links. Many sites are sources of more information than is at first apparent because they guide you to additional information via links.*

Question: Does the author or creator express opinions? If so, are they clearly labeled?

Tip: *If the creator of the Web site takes a particular stance, it should be explained within the site.*

Question: Does this site include advertising? (Is this necessarily bad?)

Tip: *Not all advertising Web sites are bad. Actually, many include quite useful information. Be careful, however; remain aware that the creator is advertising something and look at all sides of the story.*

Question: When was the Web site created? Is it obvious? When was it last updated?

Tip: *The date that the Web site was created, along with the date it was last updated, should be clearly displayed on the homepage, usually on the bottom portion.*

Question: What does this site offer that you cannot find elsewhere?

Tip: *Ideally, this format will offer new or different information, or at least a unique approach. The format allows video, photographs, visuals, and audio. View the entire Web site to ascertain why this information is particularly useful for your research.*

Question: How current are the links? Are they useful? Are they easy to navigate?

Tip: *Although the Web site itself may be current—and newly updated—that does not mean that the links are current. Check out all links and see when they were last updated. At times, creators of Web sites regularly update the site itself, but do not take the time to ensure that the links are current—or even still exist.*

Question: Is there a balance between images and text?

Tip: *Visuals and text should complement each other to explain information more thoroughly. Although a particular Web site will logically include either more visuals or more text, view the sites for balance and specified purpose.*

Question: Is the site free of grammatical errors?

Tip: *As with a print or other nonprint resources, Web sites should be grammatically correct and free of spelling errors. Blatant grammatical errors should tell you something about the accuracy and authority of the Web site.*

Exercise 6.4: Evaluating Online Resources, Revisited

Web sites differ greatly. They differ in quality, size, number of links, accuracy, esthetics, currency, to name a few ways. Examine the following Web sites on the *evaluation* of Web-based sources. Note the differences in the Web sites. Some are very interactive, some include videos and illustrations, some provide useful links, some are amateur, and some are professional. By looking at these sites, you can better determine what type of information is available on the Internet. After visiting them, consider the following:

1. Can the author(s) or creator(s) be clearly identified? If so, who are they?
2. Are the purposes of the Web site easy to identify? Are they clear and concise? What are they?
3. Why do you think the sites were produced (for example, to sell something)? How can you tell?
4. Can you determine who published the sites? Who? Where did you locate this information?
5. Is the information on the sites current? How do you know?
6. Are there any spelling or grammatical errors on the sites?

Why is it important to know all of this about Web sites? Think hard and be specific.

The Good, the Bad and the Ugly
http://lib.nmsu.edu/instruction/evalcrit.html
QUICK: The Quality Information Checklist
www.quick.org.uk/menu.htm
Criteria for Evaluation of Internet Information Resources
www.vuw.ac.nz/~agsmith/evaln
Critically Analyzing Information Sources
www.library.cornell.edu/okuref/research/skill26.htm
Information Literacy: The Web Is Not an Encyclopedia
www.oit.umd.edu/units/web/literacy/
Evaluating Web Resources
www.widener.edu/Tools_Resources/Libraries/Wolfgram_Memorial_
Library/Evaluate_Web_Pages/659/
Evaluating Internet "Research"
www.virtualsalt.com/evalu8it.htm

All types of materials can be good. But how do you choose the best tools? The following are some useful tips. Remember . . .

- Typically, a combination of approaches is best.
- There is no single best tool for a certain type of question.
- The Internet is constantly changing, and tools and information disappear without warning.
- The Internet does NOT contain all the answers!
- You cannot trust or believe everything you locate on the Internet.

CONCLUSION

All resources have the potential of being useless. Evaluate what you read; learn to discern and discriminate information—all of it—*learn to learn!* It is up to you to sift through the seemingly endless array of materials and locate those few sources that are ideal for your research. Research is not an easy task. It can, however, be an enlightening undertaking. The ability to critically assess information ultimately speeds and focuses your search, yields more pertinent resources, and significantly improves the quality of your finished product. Once you learn to locate, use, and evaluate information, you are on your way to becoming an information-literate person—one who knows how to be a lifelong learner.

When in doubt, doubt. You are fortunate to have enormous amounts of information readily available. Or are you? Because of the information explosion of the twenty-first century, it is now necessary to critically evaluate all that you read. No longer can one say that if it is in "black-and-white" is it fact.

This chapter has provided basic information regarding evaluation of print, nonprint, and Internet resources. Research in the twenty-first century requires active evaluation of materials. You must become an information-literate individual—one who knows how to find, use, and evaluate the information you need. In today's world, knowing these things will be your ticket to endless learning.

REFERENCES AND FURTHER READING

Calishain, T. 2002. "Yahoo! Service Offers More Advice Than Expertise." *Information Today*, 19: 6.
Franco, Adrienne. 2003. "Gateway to the Internet: Finding Quality Information on the Internet." *Library Trends*, 52: 228–248.
Goldsborough, R. 2002. "Can the Internet Be Trusted?" *Reading Today*, 19: 4.

Larson, Carolyn, et al. 2004. "Best Free Reference Web Sites: Sixth Annual List." *Reference & User Services Quarterly*, 44: 49–45.
Sciba, Ann. 2001. "Practice Makes Perfect (or At Least We Hope So)." *Book Report*, 20: 26–29.
Tillman, Hope N. 2001. "Evaluating Quality on the Net." Retrieved February 24, 2002, from www.hopetillman.com/findqual.html.
Trotten, Andres. 2004. "Web Searches Often Overwhelm Young Researchers." *Education Week*, 24: 8–9.

WEBLIOGRAPHY

Evaluating Information
  http://library.queensu.ca/inforef/tutorials/qcat/qeval.htm
  The Staufer Library provides an "Evaluation Checklist," "Identifying a Scholarly Article" and "Identifying a Popular Article."
Elementary CCs for Evaluating Internet Sites
  www.neutralbay-p.schools.nsw.edu.au/library/infoeval.htm
  These 22 "Cs" are adapted from the "Ten Cs for Evaluating Internet Resources."
Evaluating Web Pages: Techniques to Apply and Questions to Ask
  www.lib.berkeley.edu/TeachingLib/Guides/Internet/Evaluate.html
  This Web site discusses such issues as "What can the URL tell you?" "Scan the Perimeter of the Page," and "Look for Indicators of Quality Information."
Evaluating World Wide Web Information
  http://library.queensu.ca/inforef/tutorials/qcat/evalint.htm
The site has headings such as "Overall Content," "Compared With Other Resources," "Author," "Links," and "Interpret Address."
What Makes a Web Site Good?
  www.multcolib.org/homework/webeval.html
  This is an easy to use Web site about evaluation, created by a librarian at Multnomah County (Ore.) Library.

Chapter 7

What Should I Know About Plagiarism and Copyright?

INTRODUCTION

One of the most crucial elements of any research project is the proper recognition of the work and ideas of others. Research is a difficult and time-consuming process, and it can be tempting to simply cut and paste the information you have discovered into a document once you are done. Yet, as the past few chapters have made clear, information literacy is about more than gathering information, it is also about using it in the right way. Significantly, this involves giving credit where credit is due. Presenting the discoveries, words, or efforts of others as your own is known as *plagiarism*. A related idea that will also be discussed in this chapter is *copyright*, the legal recognition of a creator's ownership of his or her writing, art, or other work. Copyright protection allows a work's creator to restrict how that work is reproduced and distributed. While plagiarism may not always be illegal, it is never acceptable in the classroom setting. With the development of the Internet, plagiarism has become easier than ever, but learning how to avoid it is a crucial element of information literacy. As we will see in this chapter, there is nothing wrong with using someone else's ideas, research, or arguments, but it is only acceptable to do so when we remember to give credit to the originator of the material.

To get a clearer sense of why copyright is important let's imagine a personal scenario. Suppose you made a fantastic and complex drawing which you posted on an online discussion forum to show your friends. Now imagine that some other user of the forum took the drawing and posted it on another Web site under his name. This would probably make you pretty angry, wouldn't it? In the same way that you deserve to be given credit for your creative work, so too do the scholars, journalists and so on whose work you turn to while doing research. In this chapter we will discuss how to do unto the work of others what we would have them do unto ours.

PLAGIARISM

Plagiarism is not a new phenomenon. "Borrowing without permission" has been going on as long as there have been dishonest people. However, with the advent of the Internet, which provides easy access to immeasurable amounts of research materials, plagiarism has grown enormously. According to Atkins and Nelson (2001), noted authors regarding plagiarism, today millions of "computer savvy" people find it easy to plagiarize. They use someone else's intellectual property as their own without citations or credits. Often students cheat because they think everyone else does. Students are capable of changing their ways if colleges clearly demand honesty, engage students in addressing ethical issues, and put them in charge of enforcement.

Why do people plagiarize? A few reasons include

- a lack of knowledge about plagiarism,
- a lack of knowledge about information on the Internet,
- a lack of confidence in one's ability to write a paper,
- a lack of knowledge of how to cite sources, and
- procrastination.

Do any of these ring a bell?

Plagiarism is not merely copying someone else's work word-for-word. Actually, plagiarism comes in four basic forms:

1. *Exact*: Copying a source word-for-word with no credit given to the creator.
2. *Borrowing:* Turning in a paper that someone else has written (a major problem with the arrival of "paper mills" on the Internet).
3. *Unclear:* Lack of indicating where the borrowing begins and ends.
4. *Medley:* Copying of a resource using a few words here and there and not providing credit to the creator.

As you can easily see, plagiarism is a relatively simple feat—but dishonest and illegal. So, how do you keep from plagiarizing? The following are useful tips:

- Be aware of what plagiarism entails
- Allow yourself time to write the paper—do not procrastinate.
- Make certain that all research assignments are absolutely clear.
- Sharpen your time-management and planning skills.
- Learn effective research and writing skills.
- Use a variety of resources for your research (for example, Internet resources, print resources, personal interviews, etc.).
- Take notes when conducting research, writing down the full source of information.
- Conduct research using critical-thinking and problem-solving skills—moving away from the "cut and paste" mode of research.
- Write drafts and make copies of research materials.
- Cite your sources—if you are unsure, cite them anyway!
- Include an annotated bibliography (discussed in Chapter 8) with your research paper.
- Use current references (within the last two years) if your topic requires recent information.
- Include bibliography cards, note cards, photocopies of sources, and outlines with your final paper.
- Be confident in what you write—research it, study it, and reflect on it.
- Do not succumb to pressures from peers or others.
- Take pride in your work.
- Get help if you are confused or uncertain.
- Remember that you would not want someone else to "borrow" your work without giving you proper credit.

It is also helpful to learn how to perform the following and to know the difference:

1. *Paraphrase:* Restate the information in your own words. This does not require that you use quotation marks, but it does require proper citation.
2. *Summarize:* This is similar to a paraphrase, but it is shorter and even closer to your own words. Proper citation (no quotation marks) is required.
3. *Quote:* You may copy word-for-word, but this requires quotation marks and proper citation.

Internet Paper Mills

What is a *paper mill,* anyway? Paper mills allow you to directly purchase or download prewritten research papers. This is dishonest and illegal. While these monsters existed long before the Internet, with the rise of online communication the number of locations where paper mills are available has grown infinitely, and the ease with which papers can be obtained has increased immensely.

Internet paper-mill Web sites provide papers at no cost or for a fee. You should be aware, however, that instructors are now better equipped to detect use of these sites and the punishments for using them can be severe.

COPYRIGHT AND PRINT RESOURCES

Public Domain

First, it is important to understand some basic points regarding copyright. If a work is in the *public domain,* you may use it without permission. What is the public domain? It comprises all works that are not copyright protected. These works may be borrowed without permission. Examples of works in the public domain are materials produced by the United States government or older works for which copyright has expired. Remember, however, that when borrowing even these works, the author deserves credit in the form of a citation.

Creative Commons

The *Creative Commons (CC)* is a nonprofit organization devoted to expanding the range of creative work available for others to legally build upon and share. The CC Web site enables copyright holders to grant some of their rights to the public while retaining others through a variety of licensing and contract schemes, including dedication to the public domain or open-content licensing terms. The intention is to avoid the problems current copyright laws create for the sharing of information. Creative Commons provides several free licenses that copyright holders can use when releasing their works on the Web.

Fair Use

Fair use is a more complicated concept than public domain. Carol Simpson, a library science professor at the University of North Texas (Denton) and an expert in copyright issues for schools, explains, "Fair use provisions of the copyright law grant particular types of users conditional rights to use or reproduce certain copyrighted materials as long as the reproduction or use of those materials meets defined guidelines" (Simpson, 2001: 13). As stated in Section 107 of Title 17 of the U.S. Code: In determining whether the use made of a work in any particular case is a fair use the factors to be considered shall include:

- The purpose and character of the use, including whether such use is of a commercial nature or is for nonprofit educational purposes;
- The nature of the copyrighted work;
- The amount and substantiality of the portion used in relation to the copyrighted work as a whole; and
- The effect of the use upon the potential market for or value of the copyrighted work.

The fact that a work is unpublished shall not itself bar a finding of fair use if such finding is made upon consideration of all the above factors.

Remember that fair-use guidelines are exactly that—guidelines, not laws. They are merely interpretations of exceptions to copyright law agreed upon by a large number of institutions and organizations.

As Simpson (2001) notes:

> Ever since the first copyright statute was enacted, the primary focus of the law has been to protect the authors and publishers of books and other print media. Until the invention of the printing press, no one worried much about illegal copying or distribution that might injure a copyright holder. Copying was so tedious and labor-intensive there were few legal copies and fewer illegal ones. Cheap and easy mass printing made theft or misappropriation of an author's works much easier. In today's world, modern technology has made reproduction and distribution of almost any work or image nearly instantaneous (p. 21).

You might think that obtaining copyright is a difficult task. This is not the case. Under United States copyright law, anything original and creative put in a tangible form is protected by copyright—and the protection is automatic, from the moment you create something. Remember: This includes e-mail and Web pages! So, why would you bother to register a copyright application? There are three primary reasons to do so:

1. You have your copyrighted material on the public record and receive a certificate of registration.
2. You have the ability to sue. Actually, one can sue without registering; however, it makes winning lawsuits much easier if you do register.

3. In the event of a lawsuit your copyright registration will assist you with statutory damages and attorney's fees.

Let's take a look at some other questions you might be asking at this point concerning copyright issues:

Question: What works can I register for copyright protection?

Answer: *Overall, almost any original expression that is fixed in a concrete form. Examples include literary works, musical works, dramatic works, pictorial and graphic works, audiovisual works, sound recordings, architectural works, computer software, and choreography.*

Question: What is not eligible for copyright protection?

Answer: *Not many items, but the following are a few examples: facts, ideas, names, lettering, slogans, procedures, methods, concepts, short phrases, and titles.*

Question: When does copyright protection begin? When does it end?

Answer: *It begins when a work is actually created and fixed in a tangible form. Copyright protection ends after the death of the author plus 70 years. If it was published before 1923, it is not protected unless the copyright has been renewed.*

Question: What about the infamous copyright symbol?

Answer: *The symbol © is also known as copyright notice (an identifier placed on copies of a work to inform the world of copyright ownership). Today, this symbol is optional. Should you wish to use one, however, you have every right to do so, as long as you are the true author of the work.*

Question: How can one "lose" copyright?

Answer: *Essentially copyright is never lost during the copyright holder's lifetime. However, you may "give it away" (a personal choice).*

Question: Is copyright infringement really a crime?

Answer: *Yes. Although copyright law is primarily civil law, copyright violation can be a criminal act and essentially may result a possible felony conviction.*

COPYRIGHT AND NONPRINT RESOURCES

According to Simpson (2001), "Guidelines for use of audiovisual [nonprint] works vary widely. Depending on the medium and the method of acquisition, rights may vary from unlimited to short-lived. The Copyright Act of 1976 . . . clarified many ambiguities . . . " (p. 39). However, for all basic purposes, the differences in copyright law (between print and nonprint) are primarily technical and are outweighed by the similarities in the law's application.

I hope that by taking another personal look, this will become clearer for you. Suppose you are quite an artist and have created a wonderful poster. You scanned this poster and, again, placed it on your home page. Do you have copyright ownership? Yes, you have all five rights of a copyright holder. You may

1. *reproduce* (Under this right, no one other than the copyright owner may make any reproductions or copies of the work),
2. *distribute* (This right grants to the copyright holder the exclusive right to make a work available to prevent the distribution of unauthorized copies of a work),
3. *publicly perform* (This allows the copyright holder to control the public performances of the certain copyrighted works),
4. *publicly display* (This right is similar to the public performance right, except that this right controls the public display of a work), and
5. *modify the work* (This involves a type of transformation, such as the transformation of a novel into a motion picture).

As the creator of this poster, you can decide exactly how you wish it to be used. Now, what is the difference between "cannot" and "not supposed to"? Someone can print out a copy of the poster and send it to friends or display it. Is he or she supposed to? No. Why not? Because the right to do these things is reserved for the copyright holder (in this case, you).

COPYRIGHT AND INTERNET RESOURCES

Internet materials are copyrighted just as print and nonprint materials are, and notification of copyright status is not required.

Every person who writes a document published on the Internet, who creates a graphic or icon, who scans his own photograph or records his own voice into a digital file, who sends an electronic mail message, who creates a document for a newsgroup, or who designs a Web page owns the copyright to his or her creative work (Simpson, 2001: 111).

Look at it this way: If you see an item you would like to use on your

Web page, you must ask permission to use it if it is copyrighted. Therefore, if you want to use a Disney character on your Web page, you would
have to contact the Disney Corporation in order to obtain a license to
use the image. That license would tell you how you could use the Disney
character, how much you would have to pay, and other restrictions and
conditions. On the other hand, your original graphics, text, audio, etc.,
are eligible for copyright protection as soon as you place them on your
Web page.

For further information regarding this issue, visit the following Web
site:

Franklin Pierce Law Center

www.fplc.edu

*This Web site discusses copyright information for Internet authors and
artists.*

In addition, refer to "Creative Commons," discussed earlier in this
chapter.

CONCLUSION

Copyright and plagiarism are not new, but they are new issues for many
people. They are as much ethical as legal issues. It may take time to develop a strong, foolproof method to address and, eventually, prevent infringement of copyright and plagiarism. Instructors should inform you
and other students about plagiarism and copyright and address these issues in a variety of ways. It is critical that you become aware of the seri-
ousness of these problems. Students like you, who use critical thinking
and original thoughts, are less likely to infringe on copyright or plagiarize. Today's global, technological society provides many challenges; not
all of them positive. It is up to you to remain honest—to make the first
priority to *learn to learn*.

REFERENCES AND FURTHER READING

Atkins, T., and G. Nelson. 2001. "Plagiarism and the Internet: Turning the
    Tables." *English Journal* (March), 90, 101–104.

Bowman, Vibiana. 2004. *The Plagiarism Plague: A Resource Guide and CD-
    ROM Tutorial for Educators and Librarians.* New York: Neal Schuman.

Colon, Aly. 2001. "Avoid the Pitfalls of Plagiarism." *Writer,* 114: 8.

"The Credibility Question." 2004. *PC World San Francisco,* 22: 86–87.

Fialkoff, Francine, and St. Evan Lifer, (eds.). 2002. "Bringing Order to an Un-
    ruly Web." *Library Journal* (April), 127: 7.

Fisher, Julieta Dias, and Ann Hill. 2004. "Plagiarism in an Electronic Age." *Library Media Connection*, 18–19.

Heyman, J. D. et al. 2005. "Psssst . . . What's the Answer?" *People*, 63: 108–111.

Hoffman, Gretchen McCord. 2001. *Copyright in Cyberspace: Questions and Answers for Librarians*. New York: Neal-Schuman.

Horner, Jennifer. 2004. "Understanding Copyright Law." *Focus on Journals and Research* 23, 1: 6–19.

Janowski, A. 2002. "Plagiarism: Prevention, Not Prosecution." *Book Report*, 21: 2.

Laird, E. 2001. "We All Pay for Internet Plagiarism." *Education Digest*, 67: 56–59.

Lincoln, Margaret. 2002. "Internet Plagiarism." *Multimedia Schools*, 9.

McCabe, Donald. 2001, May 27. "Students' Plagiarism from Net Is Normal." *Houston Chronicle*, 5.

McCarroll, Christina. 2001, August 28. "Beating Web Cheaters at Their Own Game." *Christian Science Monitor*, 16.

Ralston, Neil. 2001. "Copyright in the Classroom." *Quill*, 89: 28.

Riedling, Ann M. 2003. "Helping Teachers Teach Students about Ethical Behavior. *Teacher Librarian*, 30: 5.

Simpson, Carol. 2001. *Copyright for Schools: A Practical Guide* (3rd ed.). Worthington, OH: Linworth.

Suarez, J., and A. Martin. 2001. "Internet Plagiarism: A Teacher's Combat Guide." *Contemporary Issues in Technology and Teacher Education* [Online serial], 1: 4. Available: http://www.citejournal.org/vol1/iss4/currentpractice/article2.htm.

Troutner, Joanne. 2002. "Plagiarism." *Teacher Librarian*, 30: 1.

Weiss, Kenneth. 2000, February 13. "Focus on Ethics Can Curb Cheating, Colleges Find." *Los Angeles Times*.

WEBLIOGRAPHY

Preventing Plagiarism

Academic Integrity
   http://sja.ucdavis.edu/a-i.htm
   This Web site offers information regarding what one can do to help prevent cheating and help make everyone's academic experience more worthwhile.
Cheating and Education
   http://7–12educators.about.com/cs/cheating/index.htm?terms=plagiarism
   This Web site is an annotated list of links about plagiarism.
Plagiarism and How to Avoid It—Lesson Plan
   http://ec.hku.hk/plagiarism/introduction.htm
   An extremely inclusive and useful site regarding how to avoid plagiarism.
Plagiarism Theme Page
   www.cln.org/themes/plagiarism.html

This site includes links about preventing, detecting, and tracking online plagiarism.

Plagiarism: What It Is and How to Recognize and Avoid It
www.indiana.edu/~wts/pamphlets/plagiarism.shtml
This Web site discusses such topics as "How Students Can Avoid Plagiarism" and "How to Recognize Unacceptable and Acceptable Paraphrases."

Information about Plagiarism

Myths about Plagiarism
www.nv.cc.va.us/home/dashkenas/PLAGIARISM.htm
This is a useful chart of myths and facts about plagiarism.

Plagiarized.com
www.plagiarized.com
This Web site discusses how the Internet can facilitate plagiarism.

Chapter 8

How Do I Give Credit to the Creator of the Information I Read?

Part of avoiding plagiarizing the work of others involves knowing how to give them credit for their work. In this chapter we will discuss *citations*, formal recognitions of credit of the work of others. There are a variety of ways to provide this information, and, in general, the most important thing is that you work to be consistent. In a classroom setting, however, you will probably be expected to cite the resource used in your papers and presentations in one of the various official styles. Different disciplines make use of different formats for citation and many academic journals require that papers submitted to them use a particular form. In this chapter, we will briefly discuss three of the most commonly used styles:

- *Chicago Manual of Style,*
- *Modern Language Association Handbook for Writers of Research Papers* (MLA), and
- *Publication Manual of the American Psychological Association Style* (APA).

Understanding how these styles work, when they are used, and how they differ from one another is yet another important part of the information literacy puzzle.

CITATION STYLES AND SOURCES

As has already been noted, numerous citation styles, both official and unofficial, exist. Most academic styles of citation require that you provide information about the author, title, publisher, and date of publication of the work you referencing. The exact information called for and the way it should be arranged in the citation is entirely dependent on the style you are using. The three styles discussed in this chapter—Chicago, MLA and APA—are all explained at greater length in manuals that describe with considerable specificity how to cite resources of different kinds. Among other things, these style manuals dictate how much information is required in each citation, how the notes should be located in the text (parenthetical references or footnotes/endnotes), and how to cite all of your resources together at the end of the paper in a bibliography.

- *Parenthetical references* are used to cite your sources within the paper itself. See Figure 8.1 for an example of how parenthetical references appear in a research paper.
- *Footnotes/endnotes* are typically used in the humanities (especially in MLA style) and include essentially the same information as parenthetical references.
- *The bibliography page* appears at the end of your paper and lists all of the sources you cited in your paper. The bibliography is arranged in alphabetical order by author, last name first. If there is no author, alphabetize by the first word of the title. The bibliography page provides all the information your readers will need if they want to find your original sources. See Figure 8.2 for an example of a bibliography page.

Research and Problem-Solving Processes and Models

Our complex global society continues to expand at a rate beyond our capacity to comprehend. Access to, comprehension, evaluation, and use of information are needed to ease the burden of change and assist humanity in navigating its course towards the future. It is imperative that students possess the skills to learn efficiently and effectively. Explicitly discussing research and problem-solving strategies makes it more likely that students will transfer these processes to future research and problem-solving situations.

The following three processes or models are widely accepted and used as problem-solving strategies in schools today: *Information Seeking* by Carol Kuhlthau, the *Big6™ Information Problem-Solving Model* by Michael Eisenberg and Robert Berkowitz, and the *Research Process* by Barbara Stripling and Judy Pitts. (Figure 1.3 on page 11 provides a brief overview of these three models.)

Carol Kuhlthau's six-stage model of the information-seeking process conceptualizes how meaning is learned through active participation with information resources. This model encourages an in-depth focus that enables students to seek more relevant information and produce a higher-quality product. Kuhlthau states, "Living in the information age requires people to go beyond the ability to locate information and requires competence in seeking meaning and understanding. More is not necessarily better without skillful guidance from an insightful person [library media specialist]" (708). (Figure 1.4 on page 11 displays this process as it relates to affective, cognitive, and sensorimotor learning.)

Another current, well-known information problem-solving model is the *Big6* approach (www.Big6.com) by Eisenberg and Berkowitz. This process describes the six thinking steps one goes through any time there is an information problem to be solved. Michael Eisenberg explains it this way: "'Brainstorm and narrow' is the essential process for information seeking strategies.... [Students should] brainstorm all possible information sources to meet the task, and then critically determine the best sources for completing the particular task" (22). (An overview of the *Big6* problem-solving model is displayed in Figure 1.5 on page 12.)

The Research Process, developed by Stripling and Pitts, connects information handling and use with subject matter that is essential for learning to occur. Stripling and Pitts discovered that students have little prior knowledge of the information-seeking process, have fragmented understandings of subject knowledge, and do not understand that their information-seeking knowledge depends on content knowledge and vice versa. As a result, school library media specialists should plan instruction specifically to assist students in attaining these skills. Learning experiences should be viewed holistically, recognizing that one area (e.g., information search process) can support other areas (e.g., content knowledge). As Judy Pitts notes, "There are many different, acceptable paths to the same end. Every...[student seemed] to have a different approach to working on a research assignment and organizing information. Each system worked well, but if everyone had been ordered to use one specific approach, many students would have found themselves incredibly frustrated" (23).

Figure 8.1   Parenthetical Reference (example). Reprinted with permission from *Reference Skills for the School Library Media Specialist: Tools and Tips,* by Ann Marlow Riedling, Linworth Publishing, 2000.

References

AASL and AECT. *Information Power: Building Partnerships for Learning.*
Chicago: American Library Association, 1988.

Eisenberg, Michael. "Big6 TIPS: Teaching Information Problem Solving:
Information Seeking Strategies." *Emergency Librarian.* 25 (1997): 22.

Katz, William. *Introduction to Reference Work: Information Sources.* 7th ed.
New York: McGraw-Hill, 1997.

Kuhlthau, Carol. "Inside the Search Process: Information Seeking from the User's
Perspectives." *Journal of the American Society for Information Science.*
42 (1991): 361-371.

Kuhlthau, Carol. "Learning in Digital Libraries: An Information Search Approach."
Library Trends. 45 (1997): 708-725.

Penland, Patrick. *Interviewing for Counselor and Reference Librarians.*
Pittsburgh, PA: University of Pittsburgh, 1970.

Pitts, Judy. "Six Research Lessons from the Other Side." *The Book Report.* 11
(1993): 22-24.

Strayer, Joseph, ed. *The ALA Glossary of Library and Information Science.*
Chicago: American Library Association, 1983.

Stripling, B. K., & Pitts, J. *Brainstorms and Blueprints: Teaching Library Research
as a Thinking Process.* Englewood, CO: Libraries Unlimited, 1988.

Whittaker, Kenneth. "Towards a Theory for Reference and Information Services."
Journal of Librarianship. 9 (1977): 49-63.

Woolls, Blanche. *The School Library Media Manager.* 2nd ed. Englewood, CO:
Libraries Unlimited, 1999.

Figure 8.2   Bibliography Page (example). Reprinted with permission from *Reference Skills for the School Library Media Specialist: Tools and Tips*, by Ann Marlow Riedling, Linworth Publishing, 2000.

With the evolution of technologies (Internet, e-mail, listservs, etc.),
methods of citing *electronic* information within the text and in the bibliography have evolved. Many people are adept at citing print resources.
However, some find it quite difficult to follow the correct form for an
Internet source. If the style manual is not current, it might not have instructions for citing the newer technologies. Usually, however, you can
find this information on the Internet. Remember, however, that elec-

tronic styles are evolving (and most likely will continue to) over time. For example, view the Web site "Citing Electronic Resources," available at www.ipl.org/ref/QUE/FARQ/netciteFARQ.html.

In addition to the information in the printed style manual, further information on each style is posted on numerous Internet sites.

Chicago Manual of Style
The *Chicago Manual of Style* can be used with all subjects and publications, although it is very often used for academic and professional scholarly and nonscholarly publications. It offers two documentation styles, one using notes and bibliographies, the other using author-date citations and reference lists. The *Chicago Manual of Style* also provides guidelines for spelling and punctuation; discusses the treatment of numbers, quotations, illustrations, tables, foreign languages, mathematical symbols, abbreviations; and explains the publishing process. In the notes and bibliography style, citations are numbered sequentially, starting with 1 in each chapter, and each citation corresponds to a numbered note containing publication information about the source cited. Although the *Chicago Manual of Style* gives some advice for documenting information from computerized data services, computer programs, and electronic documents, the information on documenting Internet sources is not complete.

The *Chicago Manual of Style* recommends italicizing certain elements (such as book and journal titles) in the printed text. According to Chicago style, the first note for a given source should include all the information necessary to identify and locate the source: the author's full name, the full title of the book, the editor's name, the place of publication, publisher, the publication date, and page numbers for quoted information. The first line of each note is indented five spaces. The *Chicago Manual of Style* has two citation styles: scientific, or author/date and reference list (for natural sciences and social sciences), and humanities, or notes and bibliographies (for fine arts and literature). Following is an example of this citation style:

Pottersfield, Stacy. *Egyptian Mummies*. San Francisco: Coo, 2006.

Exercise 8.1: Chicago Citation Style

Let's try citing using the *Chicago Manual of Style* Citation Style with the examples provided in the sites listed in the Webliography for reference. Locate one single-author book, one multiple-author book, one print periodical article, one newspaper article, one chapter from a book, one Web site, and one e-mail. Create a bibliography page with these resources, using the *Chicago Manual of Style*. Use this worksheet.

Single-author book: _____

Multiple-author book: _____

Print periodical article: _____

Newspaper article: _____

Chapter from a book: _____

Web site: _____

E-mail: _____

Modern Language Association

The *Modern Language Association* (MLA) citation style is widely used by writers in literature, language studies, and other fields in the humanities. The overall purpose of the MLA style is to allow you to keep texts as readable and as free of disruptions as possible. The *Modern Language Association Style Handbook* (or *Manual*) provides useful information regarding the purposes of research; suggestions for choosing topics; and guidance for creating outlines, bibliographies, advice on spelling, punctuation, and abbreviations.

Over 125 scholarly and literary journals, newsletters, and magazines presently use MLA guidelines. MLA style is common not only in the United States but in numerous other countries, as well. Schools and instructors have adopted the Modern Language Association style for nearly 50 years.

According to the *MLA Handbook*, each text reference to an outside source must point clearly to a specific entry in the list of works cited. The essential elements of an in-text citation are the author's name (or title of source if there is no author), and a page reference, showing where in a source cited material appears. The MLA style concerns itself with the mechanics of writing as well as proper citations. Here is an example of this citation style. Note that MLA recommends underlining rather than italics.

Caples, Rose. <u>The Unnoticed Child</u>. New York: Neal-Schuman, 2006.

 Exercise 8.2: Modern Language Association Citation Style

Now let's give MLA a try. Locate one multiple-author book, one Web site, one listserv, one online journal article, one print newspaper article. Using the Modern Language Association style and the sites in the Webliography for reference, create a bibliography of your resources. Record your results on this worksheet:

Multiple-author book: _____

Web site: _____

Listserv: _____

Online journal article: _____

Print newspaper article: _____

American Psychological Association
The *Publication Manual of the American Psychological Association* (APA) provides documentation advice for writers in the social sciences. It discusses manuscript content and organization, writing style, and manuscript preparation. The APA *Publication Manual* provides hundreds of guidelines about how to format references, statistics, tables, punctuation, and grammar. It also contains writing tips and instructions on formatting manuscripts. APA style focuses on the needs of presenting psychological information. It omits general rules explained in widely available style books and examples of usage that have little relevance to the behavioral and social sciences. Here is an example of this citation style:

Sterling, D. (2005). *Laptops of the future.* Chicago: Avi.

See Exercise 8.3.

Exercise 8.3: American Psychological Association Citation Style

Take a look at either the APA manual or some of the APA info sites listed in the Webliography. Are you ready to try the American Psychological Association (APA) Style? OK. Locate one single-author book, one no-author book, one online journal article, one print journal article, and one e-mail. Using APA style, create a reference list page using your resources.

This worksheet may assist you with this task:
Single-author book:
No-author book:
Online journal article:
Print journal article:
E-mail:

THE ANNOTATED BIBLIOGRAPHY

Bibliographies have been the topic of this entire chapter. There may be times, however, when you will be required to create an annotated bibliography. What is an annotated bibliography? It is an organized list of sources or citations with a brief note or description (annotation) about each item. So, what is the function of an annotated bibliography? Depending on the context, an annotated bibliography can serve a number of purposes.

- It reviews the literature on a specific topic.
- It illustrates the quality of your research.
- It informs the reader of the relevance, accuracy, and quality of the sources cited.
- It provides examples of available resources.
- It explores the topic for further research.

Good annotated bibliographies provide comprehensive coverage of the issues studied. By definition, they are extensive and exhaustive in the treatment of their topics. When exploring an issue, annotated bibliographies will look at the pros and cons of a subject matter. By reclassifying literature based on its point of view, an annotated bibliography provides students with relevant information. In addition, annotated bibliographies save precious research time by providing one-stop shopping. When carefully organized and logically presented, they can be a valuable service with their added value—evaluation and synthesizing of information.

Annotations are descriptive and critical; they expose the author's (your) point of view, clarity and appropriateness of expression, and authority. Typically, an annotation is no more than 150 words and follows the bibliographic citation. Each style (APA, MLA, Chicago, etc.) has its own specific procedure for writing bibliographic annotations (see your style manual). The following is an example of an annotated bibliography using fictitious citations and annotations and APA style.

Smith, J. R. (2001). The erosion of traditional family rituals among adolescents. *Psychology Today, 40,* 44–48.

The author, a researcher with Rutgers University, uses information from surveys of adolescents to test his hypothesis that traditional family rituals among adolescents are not considered "important." He finds his hypothesis strongly supported by both male and female adolescents. In contrast, an earlier study by Jones (cited above) shows that males and females differ greatly in the importance they place on family rituals, with females believing it is vitally important.

Tell, J. O. (2002). Happy days are here again! *American Sociological Review, 101,* 444–450.

Tell explains that adolescents are "happier and more well adjusted" today than they were 50 years ago. He attributes this to their early independence as well as to the support they receive from peers. I do not agree with Tell's opinion, but I believe it is important to consider all points of view.

Exercise 8.4: Annotated Bibliography

Your teacher has requested that you locate five online articles from a periodical database on any topic(s). Read the articles and create annotations for each of the five using APA citation style.

1.
2.
3.
4.
5.

CONCLUSION

The overall purpose of citing sources in a research paper is to provide credit to the creator(s) of the information and to give the reader(s) of your paper access to the information they need to locate your original sources. There are numerous citation styles and manuals, but three basic citation styles are *Chicago Manual of Style, MLA Handbook for Writers of Research Papers,* and the *Publication Manual of the American Psychological Association.* Printed manuals and Internet sites can assist you in learning how to cite your sources properly both within the text (parenthetical references), in footnotes and endnotes, and in the bibliography page. Citing sources properly is an essential aspect of research.

REFERENCES AND FURTHER READING

Bauman, M. Garrett. 2001, November 9. "The Devilments of Style." *The Chronicle of Higher Education:* B5.

The Chicago Manual of Style (15th ed.). 2003. Chicago, IL: The University of Chicago Press.

Crane, Beverly E. 2000. *Teaching with the Internet: Strategies and Modes for K–12 Curricula.* New York: Neal-Schuman.

Gibaldi, Joseph. 2003. *MLA Handbook for Writers of Research Papers* (6th ed.). New York: Modern Language Association of America.

Harmon, Charles. 2000. *Using the Internet, Online Services, and CD-ROMs for Writing Research and Term Papers* (2nd ed.). New York: Neal-Schuman.
Junion-Metz, Gail. 2004. "The Biblio-Files." *School Library Journal*, 7: 24–25.
Junion-Metz, Gail. 2004. "Footnotes for the Confused." *School Library Journal*, 8: 24–25.
Lane, Nancy, Margaret Chisolm, and Carolyn Mateer. 2000. *Techniques for Student Research: A Comprehensive Guide to Using the Library*. New York: Neal-Schuman.
Publication Manual of the American Psychological Association (5th ed.). 2001. Washington, DC: American Psychological Association.

WEBLIOGRAPHY

APA Citation Style

APA Style: Reference Examples for Electronic Source Materials
www.apastyle.org/elecsource.html
This Web site offers examples of citations to various electronic resources using APA style.
The Writing Center: APA Documentation
www.wisc.edu/writetest/Handbook/DocAPA.html
This is an all-inclusive Web site on the use of APA citation style.

MLA Citation Style

OWL at Purdue University: Using Modern Language Association (MLA) Format
http://owl.english.purdue.edu/handouts/research/r_mla.html
This is a very inclusive Web site for using MLA citation style.
The Writing Center: MLA Documentation
www.wisc.edu/writetest/Handbook/DocMLA.html
This is an all-inclusive Web site on the use of MLA citation style.

Chicago Citation Style

Chicago Manual of Style
http://www.press.uchicago.edu/Misc/Chicago/cmosfaq/cmosfaq.html
This site answers new questions about the 15th edition of the Chicago Manual of Style.

Citation Styles—Generally Speaking

ONLINE! Citation Styles: Index
www.bedfordstmartins.com/online/citex.html
This Web site is extremely useful for learning how to cite specific resources using both APA and MLA citation styles.
Style Guides and Resources on the Internet
www.ifla.org/I/training/citation/citing.htm
This is a list of links to useful citation style guides and resources.

Style Sheets for Citing Resources (Print & Electronic)
www.lib.berkeley.edu/TeachingLib/Guides/Internet/Style.html
This Web site covers a wealth of information regarding plagiarism and citation styles.

Chapter 9

Now That I've Finished the Research, How Do I Write the Paper?

INTRODUCTION

In the previous chapters we have covered a lot of information-literacy ground, from developing a topic to gathering materials to giving credit for the information you have found. Ideally, your school work will have benefited from these chapters as your research skills have improved. Nevertheless, no matter how good your research is, you will never be able to do anything with it if you can't organize it properly. Actually, organizing information is important in many aspects of your life. For example, let's say you are going to have a party for your friends. You would need to organize an invitation list, what you will have to eat, what music you will play, and so forth. In much the same way that you need a plan for your party if you want it to be a hit, you will need to plan out your papers and presentations if you want them to be interesting, fun, and comprehensible.

Some of the groundwork for what will be discussed in this chapter has already been covered in this book. In Chapter 2, for example, we talked about shaping your thesis statement, a crucial step for staying focused as you go about completing your work. Here we will go further, discussing how to turn your research and ideas into an outline and a rough draft. Last, we will consider how to put the final touches on your work. We will look at editing strategies, presentation formats, and other means of making your work shine. As you read, remember that information literacy is about more than knowing what to look for and where to find it; it is also about putting your work in a form that can be understood by others.

ORGANIZATION OF INFORMATION

As you probably know, the endpoint of almost all research done for classes is some form of research project. Such projects can take on many forms, but the point is always to find the best possible way to demonstrate that which you have learned. Ideally, a research project should bring together material acquired from a variety of sources into one coherent whole. Whatever style you use, try to bring together the information you want to convey in a manner that is easily and immediately comprehensible. Sometimes it is helpful to work from a basic organizational format of some kind; especially if this helps you keep your thoughts flowing. Keep the example of the party above in mind: If you manage the details of your work with care you can be sure that it will achieve its intended effect. Among other things, be sure to balance your project so that it is both general enough to draw in your audience and specific enough to teach them something new.

Though it may seem surprising, one of the first steps of organization begins before you even start to put your project together. As you go about looking for information, be sure to always write the information about your sources in case you use them in your final project. There are few things worse than setting out to write a paper, only to realize that you have no idea where you found your information.

The citation should include

- author or creator's name,
- title of the resource,
- place of publication,
- publisher's name,
- date of copyright (year only for books; date, month for newspapers),
- volume and issue number for journals,
- page numbers,
- URL (if applicable) and date accessed.

This will save time, because you will not waste it relocating materials to get this information. In addition, it is important to take notes about each source you locate. Answer questions such as the following:

- Does this material fit the topic?
  Relevance is vital. For instance, if your topic is violence in schools and you locate a resource about a specific street gang in New York in the early 1900s, does that fit your topic?
- Is it a scholarly resource?
  Scholarly means written by an expert in the field. If you locate information on the Internet written by someone you cannot find information about, is that information necessarily scholarly?
- Is the information in this source accurate?
  This might take some work. Go to a few other resources and see if they have the same information. If your source differs, it may not be accurate.
- Are there any notable biases in the material?
  Remember, many organizations place information on the Internet place that is biased toward their cause. For example, do you think the beef association of America is going to be pro-chicken?
- Why do I want to use this resource; where will it fit into my research project?
  There are a number of reasons to use a resource—for scholarly information, to show a particular point of view, and so forth. Be certain that you are not using the resource because it was easy to find or you liked the format.

Carry a notebook around with you and write all information down right away. You can later turn it into a word document or enter it into a database. Always paraphrase or summarize the information, stating it in your own words. There are many different kinds of summaries, and they vary according to the degree with which you interpret the resource. Some are pages long, others just one or two sentences. However, for all types of summaries, you are responsible for generally stating the ideas of another writer in your own words. In order to summarize or paraphrase, it is important to

- read the original text very carefully and
- highlight or underline what you believe are the main points.

It is also helpful to use the author's last name as a "tag" to introduce information, such as, "Jones contends that. . . . " As a reminder, keep in mind that if you copy and use the information word-for-word, you need to place quotation marks around it.

Outlining

According to the OWL Online Writing Lab an outline is:

- A logical, general description
- A schematic summary
- An organizational pattern
- A visual and conceptual design of your writing

The specific purposes of an outline are to:

- Help you organize your ideas
- Present your material in a logical form
- Show the relationships among ideas in your writing
- Define boundaries and groups.

Before you begin, your process is to:

- Determine the purpose of your paper
- Determine the audience you are writing for
- Develop the thesis of your paper, and then
- Brainstorm
- Organize
- Order and
- Label (owl.english.purdue.edu).

An outline provides an overview of your paper and allows you to quickly see missing elements, irrelevant items, and the structure of your project. It will help keep your paper organized and focused, and cut down on the number of rough drafts you generate. The following steps are help-ful when constructing your outline:

- Once you have decided on a subject, brainstorm your ideas by writing down any facts, thoughts, and insights you have. In order to get started brainstorming, ask yourself questions. How does the topic affect you or others? One of the tricks to effective brainstorming to the think logically about the topic, considering as much as possible about it. If you are having trouble generating ideas, ask someone else to discuss the topic with you and ask you questions.
- Work on organizing your introductory paragraph by answering the following questions: Who? What? When? Where? Why? and How?
- Organize your beginning paragraph by listing points to be made in

each sentence. Begin with the most general, gradually getting more and more specific, until you make your very specific thesis statement.

- Using the thesis statement, list categories for the paragraphs in the body of your paper.
- Plan your conclusion, which is the reverse order of the introduction.

Remember, writing a paper is a "process." The first step in this process is to develop a thorough outline and follow it. Also, refer to your thesis statement over and over to make sure you stay on topic.

A *working outline* might be only an informal list of topics and sub-topics that you are thinking of covering in your paper. A *final outline* should enhance the organization and coherence of your research paper. If portions of your outline seem weak in comparison to others, more research may be required to create a sense of balance. Outlines should be organized according to your purposes. Are you trying to show the chronology of some historical development, the cause-and-effect relationship between one phenomenon and another, the process by which something is accomplished, or the logic of some position? Regardless of type of research paper, attempt to bring related material together under general headings and arrange sections so that they relate logically to each other. A final outline can be written as a *topic outline*, in which you use only short phrases to suggest ideas, or as a *sentence outline*, in which you use full sentences to show the development of ideas more fully. Your outline will differ with the type of research paper you are writing. Overall, however, it is best to bring related resources together under common headings and organize divisions so they relate understandably to each other.

 Exercise 9.1: Outlining

Pick a specific topic, such as "High School Sports and Steroids," about which you already know a great deal and follow the outlining procedure above to create an appropriate outline.

The Rough Draft

Writing a rough draft is a late stage in the writing process. Before you get to this stage, be certain that you have done a great deal of preparation: clarified your topic, taken lots of notes, collected as many ideas in writing as you can, and so forth. Plan to finish your rough draft a day or two before your paper is due so you will have time to revise it. The following are helpful tips regarding rough drafts:

- Gather all of the materials you will need, including notes, books, articles, partial drafts, computer, and any other materials.
- Set aside a substantial period of time (2 to 3 hours) to get started.
- Develop your thesis. Write one or two paragraphs in your own words explaining the main point of your paper. Remember, your paper should be written to support and develop your thesis.
- Create an outline.
- Visualize your reader. As you write, speak to your reader or audience.
- Tell your story quickly. Don't think you must start with your introduction. Write quickly, using whatever words come easily to you. Don't worry about grammar or spelling. Don't try to impress. Just be yourself on paper. Work for short periods of time and take a break.
- Include all of your ideas and information in the rough draft. You can revise or remove irrelevant information later.
- Double or triple space so you will have room to make changes.

Revision

You will look at your work with a more critical eye if you wait a few hours or a day between finishing the rough draft and revising your paper. Think about the following when you are reviewing your rough draft:

- Does your introduction help the reader to know what he or she will be reading?
- Do your ideas flow logically?
- Does your conclusion summarize the main points and offer new insight on the topic?
- Have you found any grammatical errors, such as sentence structure, spelling, and punctuation that will detract from the quality of your paper?
- Have you included a bibliography using the citation style required, and have you cited your sources correctly within the text of your paper?
- Are you keeping an extra copy of your paper (on a floppy disk, flash drive, or CD)?

It is also helpful to follow these research tactics (many of these are merely reminders):

- Develop your personal search strategy and stick with it.
- Keep all of your notes in one folder and label the folder with your name, the title of your research project, and the date.
- Ask for assistance if you need it.
- Always evaluate your resources (print and electronic).
- Paraphrase/summarize all information (you will understand it better later if it is in your own words).
- Keep narrowing your search if necessary.
- Use a wide variety of resources.
- Use scholarly sources as much as possible.
- Always keep copyright and plagiarism in mind.
- Have someone else look at your resources, outline, and rough draft.
- Remember that research and writing is not linear; it is a *circular process*. While you are writing you may discover again and again that more research is required.

Regardless of how you organize information, you must maintain a systematic approach with which you are comfortable.

IMPROVING YOUR WRITING

Anyone can learn to write better, but it requires time and work. Even a small effort toward improvement can have positive results. The following are several tips to improve your writing ability:

- Take what you are doing seriously. Good writing is important.
- Read—anything and everything you can, whenever you can. The more familiar and comfortable you are with reading and writing, the easier it will become.
- Try to improve your vocabulary. Make it a point to learn a few new words every week or month. A wide vocabulary gives you a better command of the language and more possibilities for expressing your ideas to others. It may be helpful to visit the following Web site: Dictionary.com Word of the Day
    http://dictionary.reference.com/wordoftheday
- Practice writing—letters to friends, a journal—any way you can think of. Practice makes perfect!
- Learn to revise your writing to become clearer and more focused.
- Use a dictionary and thesaurus. If you do not know a word, be sure to look it up.
- Control your language—do not let it control you.

- Read what you write aloud. Your ears can tell you much about how you write.
- Simplify and simplify more. Eliminate anything unnecessary.
- Think clearly. When you are tired or distraught, things become fuzzy and unclear. Choose appropriate times to write.
- Avoid writer's block by understanding that it takes time and patience to be a good writer.

THE FINISHING TOUCHES

You have written your paper—or so you think—but don't stop now. No matter how many times you read a paper on the computer, you are likely to miss many of your errors. It is helpful to take a break between writing and final proofreading. It is also useful to read your paper aloud—so that you read every little word. In addition, sliding a blank sheet of paper down the page as you read encourages you to make a detailed review of your paper. Even the best writers cannot be totally objective about their own work. Therefore, it is wise to do the following:

- Have someone else (or several others) read your paper and provide you with feedback.
- Proofread your paper—several times.
- Edit and write your final revisions.

It might be helpful to think of this in terms of someone else evaluating your work. The "best" work should

- contain a beginning, middle, and end;
- include an introduction that is clear, focused, complete, and strong, and requires critical-thinking skills;
- show evidence of organization and revision;
- use a variety of carefully selected resources;
- contain information that is supported in numerous and diverse sources;
- be original and written with accuracy, detail, and understanding;
- be free of grammatical errors of all types (spelling, punctuation, consistency of tense, avoidance of clichés, verb agreement, no fragments or run-on sentences, etc.);
- include a conclusion that is strong and concise; and
- use proper citations within the text and on the bibliography page (according to the required citation style).

PRESENTING YOUR RESEARCH

Your research paper is a compilation of the essential facts and ideas on a topic that have been gathered from a variety of resources. The information collected about your research topic should be presented from *your* perspective. This will make your research project an original, creative presentation of a familiar body of information. There are numerous ways to present a paper, using various resources and equipment. How you will present the paper may depend on a number of factors, for example:

- Amount of time permitted (*If there were 30 presentations to be made in a 60-minute class period, you obviously would not opt for a PowerPoint presentation or a play.*)
- Resources and materials available (*It would be hard to show Internet sites on a screen if the room had no way to connect to the Internet.*)
- Size of the audience (*For example, it would be difficult to present to an audience of 300 using posters.*)
- Size and arrangement of the room (*If the room was small and cramped, performing a play would not be a smart idea.*)
- Constraints imposed by the delivery medium or audience (*It would be highly inappropriate to play the guitar to promote a new type of hearing device.*)
- Type of information being communicated (*It would be inappropriate to use song and dance to advertise a new antidepressant medication.*)
- Expertise and background of the audience (*It would not be appropriate to put on a puppet show to promote a new heart transplant technique to top surgeons across the country.*)
- Manner in which the audience is expected to use the information (*It would not be very effective to tell people how to use a new computer program—a hands-on method, or at least visuals, would be more suitable.*)

In addition, your particular topic may lend itself better to one method than another. Physical information (such as location) is often best communicated graphically; graphics are also better suited to conveying information about individual objects. For example, if your research topic is bats, it might be useful to use visuals to show how bats sleep and the features of their wings.

Outlines are useful tools in planning *and delivering* a presentation. A *planning outline* helps in determining the organizational sequence that makes the most sense for presenting a particular topic to a given audience. It is more detailed in that it not only labels the parts, but it also describes subpoints and shows relationships between major ideas. A *presentation outline* assists you during the presentation. It is much briefer than a planning outline because its purpose is only to provide cues that help you "stay on track" during the presentation. Regardless of the presentation type, all presentations should accomplish the following:

- They should present the research information in a logical, interesting sequence that the audience can follow.
- They should provide information that is accurate, clear, and appropriate.

If visuals are included, be certain that the graphics reinforce the research, that the visual information is accurate, and that the graphics are large and clear enough for everyone to see. If you use video or audio, be certain that they enrich the presentation and convey meaning without being too lengthy. Also, remain cognizant of the need for smooth transitions. Transitions are like bridges between parts of your presentation. Pause during a transition, and choose your words carefully. For example, if you are showing comparison, use words such as "in contrast" or "compared to." It is sometimes useful to repeat yourself, using phrases such as "as I have noted previously." Examples are also useful; if you use an example, preface it with "for instance" or "to illustrate." Finally, to summarize or conclude a presentation, use phrases such as "on the whole" or "in conclusion." If you are presenting orally, use a clear voice and pronounce terms correctly and precisely. In addition, maintain as much eye contact with the audience as possible.

Exercise 9.2: Presentations

To get some experience presenting your work, pair off with another student. Each of you should pick a topic about which you think you know a considerable amount. Take a few minutes to prepare an outline of the key points that you think everyone should know about this topic and then give a one-minute verbal explanation of this information to your partner. Each of you should then explain to the other where you think more background or information might be needed in your partner's talk.

After you have done this, go off on your own again and develop your list of points more fully, using your partner's comments to help fill out your outline. As soon as you feel ready, meet up with your partner again and give a second presentation, this time of five minutes.

What did you learn from this experience? How might this practice session help you give better presentations in the future?

CONCLUSION

Effective organization of information is critical to a high-quality research paper. Develop an organizational plan with which you are comfortable. Remember to create an outline first, followed by a rough draft. Before finalizing your paper, proofread it, have others read it, then edit and revise. Beginning to write a research paper is the most difficult part, and organization is the key to success. Presentation of your final paper should be "the icing on the cake." This is your opportunity to show others what you have accomplished.

Your research project is finished! You have now learned the process—from beginning to end—of creating and presenting a research paper. You are information literate and have *learned to learn.*

FURTHER READING

Deutsch, Laura. 2004. "With a Little Help from My Friends." *Writing,* 2: 14–16.
Hoff, David J. 2001. "Well-Crafted Assignments Key to Good Writing, Researchers Find." *Education Week,* 42: 5–11.
Kreyche, Gerald F. 2005, March 1. "Speak without Fear." *USA Today Magazine,* 2718: 81–82.

Montante, Sarah. 2004. "Good Writers Weren't Born That Way." *Literacy Cavalcade*, 7: 36–38.

Thompson, Helen M. 2005. "Ideas, Information, and Organization: Connecting Information Literacy and Writing." *School Library Media Activities Monthly*, 7: 48–51.

WEBLIOGRAPHY

Outlining

Getting Started: Outlining
http://grammar.ccc.commnet.edu/grammar/composition/brainstorm_outline.htm
This useful Web site offers a wealth of information on outlining.

Outlining
www.eths.k12.il.us/manual_of_form_and_style/outlining.html
This extremely helpful site includes purposes, types, and rules of outlining.

Outlining Software: An Essential Tool for Brainstorming, Business Planning and Writing
www.innovationtools.com/Articles/ArticleDetails.asp?a=107
This site discusses electronic outlining and how it has assisted students.

OWL at Purdue University: Developing an Outline
http://owl.english.purdue.edu/handouts/general/gl_outlin.html
This Web site discusses a wide variety of aspects of outlining.

SchwabLearning.org—Outlining
www.schwablearning.org/articles.asp?r=484&g=4
This is a useful site regarding all aspects of outlining—especially for students with learning disabilities.

Editing and Proofreading

Editing and Proofreading
www.unc.edu/depts/wcweb/handouts/proofread.html
This site provides tips and strategies for revising writing.

Proofreading
www.ucc.vt.edu/stdysk/proofing.html
This Web site explains that proofreading is an acquired skill and includes exercises.

Public Speaking

How to Conquer Public Speaking Fear
www.stresscure.com/jobstress/speak.html
This is a special report to help take the stress out of public speaking.

Public Speaking and Speech Writing
www.speechtips.com
This Web site includes tips for speaking at a variety of engagements.

A Research Guide for Students: Presentation Tips for Public Speaking
www.aresearchguide.com/3tips.html
This site offers numerous useful tips for effective public speaking.

Rough Drafts

Checklist for Rough Draft
http://faculty.plattsburgh.edu/gary.kroll/courses/his285/checklist_for_rough_draft.htm
This site offers a checklist for a rough draft that a professor used in an undergraduate course.
Tips for Writing a Rough Draft
www.arc.sbc.edu/roughdraft.html
This Web site discusses freewriting, brainstorming, and other issues concerned with rough drafts.

Organizing Information

A+ Research and Writing Links: Organizing Information
www.ipl.org/div/teen/aplus/linksorganizing.htm
This Web site discusses "Taking Notes," "Outlining" and "Organizing Information by Cubing, Mapping and More."
Site Design: Organizing Information
www.webstyleguide.com/site/organize.html
The site refers to organization as it applies to Web sites.

Glossary

Abstract: A brief summary of a book, article, or Web site.

Annotated Bibliography: It is an organized list of sources or citations with a brief note or description (annotation) about each item.

Annotation: A paragraph for each information source cited in a bibliography that summarizes the important findings and conclusions in that source.

APA: (American Psychological Association): A citation style that is used most often by writers and students in the sciences and social sciences.

Bias: Prejudice; an inclination or preference that inhibits impartiality.

Bibliography: A list of the resources you use when researching your paper.

Boolean Logic: A way to combine terms using "operators" such as AND, OR, and NOT. AND requires that all terms appear in a record. OR retrieves records with either term. NOT excludes terms.

Browser: A software program that makes it possible to view World Wide Web documents. It translates HTML-encoded files into the text, images, sounds, and other feature you see. Examples are Netscape and Internet Explorer.

Call Number: Letters and numbers assigned to a book according to its subject to indicate its location on the shelf.

CD-ROM: The acronym for Compact Disc-Read Only Memory. Computer storage discs that can contain vast amounts of information.

Chicago Manual of Style: A citation style that can be used primarily for scholarly publications.

Citations: Brief publication information about a book, article, Web site, and or other resource. Citations usually include the author, title, publisher, and copyright date.

Citing: The process of giving credit to the information sources used to write a paper or develop a presentation.

Collaboration: To work jointly with others, especially in an intellectual endeavor.

Copyright: Legal ownership of a work that provides the creator of a work the sole right to publish and sell that work.

Critical Thinking Skills: Higher-level thinking skills that include analysis and synthesis of ideas.

Cross Reference: A direction from one term or heading to another. A SEE reference indicates that all materials will be found listed under another specific term; a SEE ALSO reference lists other terms under which related materials might be found.

Deep (or Invisible) Web: Content that is stored in databases accessible on the Web, but not available via search engines.

Dewey Decimal Classification System (DDC): A classification system used primarily in school and public libraries that is based on ten main classes.

Directory: A directory is a system that a computer uses to organize files on the basis of specific information. Directories can be organized hierarchically so that files can appear in a number of different ways, such as the order in which they were created, alphabetically by name or by type, and other ways.

Domain: A scheme for indicating logical and sometimes geographical venues of a Web page from the network. Examples are .edu (education), .com (commercial), .gov (government).

Edition: All copies of a book printed from one typesetting without substantial change. A revised edition is a corrected and updated edition based on the original with modifications.

Editor: The person responsible for compiling and organizing a periodical or a book written by several authors.

Endnote: A note placed at the end of an article, chapter, or book that comments or cites a reference for a designated part of the text.

Fair Use: Fair use grants particular types of users conditional rights to use or reproduce certain copyrighted materials if the reproduction or use meets specific guidelines.

Final Outline: Similar to a working outline, but containing more complete information on the research topic.

Focus: A central theme within a topic.

Footnote: A note placed at the bottom of a page of a book or manuscript that comments on or cites a reference for a designated part of the text.

Full-Text: The complete text of a book, article, or Web site.

Handbook: A reference work that serves as a handy guide to a particular subject.

HTML: Hypertext Markup Language. This is a standardized language of computer code, imbedded in "source" documents behind all Web documents, containing the textual content, images, links to other documents, and formatting instructions for display on the screen.

Hypertext: On the World Wide Web this feature allows a text area, image, or other object to become a "link" (like a chain) that retrieves other computer files on the Internet.

Independent Learning: Learning information without the assistance of others.

Indexes: Something that serves to guide, point out, or otherwise facilitate reference.

Intellectual Freedom: Intellectual Freedom is the right of every individual to both seek and receive information from all points of view without restriction.

Interlibrary Loan: A cooperative agreement among libraries willing to share their books and other resources with each other.

Internet: A network that connects computers worldwide.

Internet Paper Mill: A Web site that allows you to directly purchase or download research papers online.

Introduction: The first part of a research paper that introduces the audience to the subject about which the paper is being written.

Journal: A scholarly or professional periodical.

Keyword: A word searched for in a search command. Keywords are searched in any order.

Librarian's Index: A subject directory that is compiled by library experts.

Library Catalogs (also called OPACs): An organized and searchable record of all the materials that a particular library owns.

Library of Congress Classification System (LC): A classification system used in large (primarily public and academic libraries) to arrange their materials.

Library Policies and Procedures: Critical documents to help assure that libraries can operate efficiently and effectively and to protect and assist all library users.

Lifelong Learners: People who know how to learn without assistance. This applies to all individuals, not merely students, over the span of their lives.)

Link: The URL imbedded in another document, so that if you click on the highlighted text or button referring to the link, you retrieve the outside URL.

Match-All Search: This type of search is similar to Boolean searching, but in place of AND a plus sign (+) is used; in place of NOT a minus sign (-) is used.

Meta-Search Engine: These are search engines that automatically submit your keyword search to several other search tools and retrieve results from all their databases.

MLA (Modern Language Association): A citation style that is most often used by writers and students in the humanities, languages, and literature disciplines.

OPAC (Online Public Access Catalog): This is a general term for a library's electronic catalog.

Outline: An outline provides an overview of your research and allows you to quickly see missing elements, irrelevant items, and the structure of your project.

Paraphrase: Re-wording or summarizing someone else's words or ideas.

Parenthetical References: Writing sources cited on your bibliography page within the paper itself.

Peer Review: Process in which experts in the field read, review, and evaluate articles based on certain criteria before recommending them for publication.

Periodical: Any information source that is issued regularly, for example, daily, weekly, monthly, or quarterly. This includes newspapers, magazines, and journals.

Periodical Database: A searchable index to periodicals, such as news papers, magazines, and journals.

Personal (Home) Page: A Web page created by an individual, as opposed to a page created for an institution, business, organization, or other entity.

Phrase Searching: A type of search that uses more than one keyword enclosed in quotations (" "). It is sometimes called a character string.

Plagiarism: The act of copying or paraphrasing someone else's text or ideas without giving them credit.

Preface: A section of a book that includes the purpose, scope, and organization. The preface tells why the book was written and what is to come next in the text.

Protocol: This is the standard or set of rules that two computers use to communicate with each other. Also known as a communications protocol or network protocol, a set of such standards ensures that different network products or programs can work together. Any product that uses a given protocol should work with any other product using the same protocol.

Public Domain: A storehouse of all works that are not protected by copyright.

Reference Material: A book or other work designed to be consulted rather than read completely; generally a source that must be used within a library.

Robot (or Spider): A program designed to automatically go out and explore the Internet for a specific purpose. Robots that record and index all of the contents of the network to create searchable databases are sometimes called *spiders*. WebCrawler and Lycos are examples of robots.

Rough Draft: A first attempt at writing a research paper.

Scope: The breadth and depth of what is covered and in what detail in a resource.

Search Engine: An automated, controlled system that enables users to search for Web pages on a selected topic by entering keywords.

Search Statement: A set of instructions or a group of keywords used to locate appropriate information.

Sentence Outline: An outline that uses full sentences to show the development of ideas more fully.

Serial: Any publication issued on an ongoing basis, usually published at regular intervals and intended to be continued indefinitely. A periodical is one type of serial.

Social Responsibility: In an information literacy context, the understanding that access to information is basic to the functioning of a democracy; one who realizes that equitable access to information from a range of sources and in all formats is a fundamental right in a democracy.

Subject Directory: A human-controlled system that enables users to browse through subject categories for information.

Subject Heading: A word or group of words under which all materials on a particular topic are listed in a card catalog, OPAC, or in an index.

Summarize: Similar to paraphrase, but provides information even closer to your own words than the words of the author or creator.

Synonyms: Two or more words or expressions that have the same, or nearly the same, meaning in some or all senses.

Thesaurus: A book of words and their synonyms.

Thesis Statement: The narrow conclusion you make based on the information gathered for a research paper. It is an assertion; not a statement of fact.

Title Page: Typically the first page in a book that tells the author, title, illustrator, and publisher.

Title Searching: A search method that allows one to search with the HTML title of a Web page.

Topic Outline: An outline that uses only short phrases to suggest ideas.

Truncation: A search technique using a symbol (usually an asterisk) at the end of a word in order to retrieve all of its possible endings.

URL (Universal Resource Locator): This is the most basic information about where a Web page is located on the World Wide Web. It includes information about what Web server the page is stored, in which directory it is located, its name, and the protocol used to retrieve it.

Verso Page: The page on the reverse side of the title page that includes information such as the copyright date, author, title, publisher, and other aspects of publication.

Virtual Library: A managed collection of information resources and services available electronically via the Internet.

Volume: An individual book; whatever is found in one binding. For a periodical, a volume is the collective unit for a set of issues. Frequently a volume is one year's worth of issues.

Webliography: A list of Web sites including the name and URL of the Web site that were used in or relate to, for example, a chapter in a book.

Wildcards: A search technique that typically uses the question mark symbol in place of a letter in a word.

Working Outline: An informal list of topics and subtopics associated with a research paper.

WWW (The World Wide Web): A portion of the Internet that presents textual and multimedia information in page format.

Yahoo!: Currently the largest and most well-known subject directory.

Index

About the Author

Ann Marlow Riedling is a graduate of Indiana University with a bachelor's degree in education, graduate of the University of Georgia with a master's degree in library science and educational technology; and a graduate of the University of Louisville with a doctorate in educational administration and information technology. She has worked in library science, education, and educational technology since 1974. Ann has published eight previous textbooks and tradebooks. She served the academic year 1999/2000 as a Fulbright Scholar in Bahrain, Yemen, and Egypt, teaching and consulting in information science. She spent 2005 as a Fulbright Scholar in Oman, teaching medical librarianship. Her areas of research and interest include distance education, information literacy, young adult literature, and school reference services.